AMERICAN MAVERICK
IN JAPAN

AMERICAN MAVERICK IN JAPAN

◆

"The Rick Roa Story"

As told to Tony Teora

iUniverse, Inc.

New York Lincoln Shanghai

AMERICAN MAVERICK IN JAPAN
"The Rick Roa Story"

iUniverse, Inc.

For information address:
iUniverse, Inc.
2021 Pine Lake Road, Suite 100
Lincoln, NE 68512
www.iuniverse.com

ISBN: 0-595-31428-7 (pbk)
ISBN: 0-595-76363-4 (cloth)

Printed in the United States of America

Contents

ACKNOWLEDGEMENTS

There are just too many of my friends to name in this book,
but I want to tell you all:

"Thanks for the memories."

If I left you out, what can I say except: "I love you all."

SPECIAL ACKNOWLEDGMENTS

To Tony Teora: "Without you, this would never have been written—Thanks buddy."

To Pete Heyrman and Ruth Turner: "I want to thank Peter Heyrman and Ruth Turner of Bear Press Editorial Services for their editing on this project."

COVER DESIGN

The front cover photo was taken by Randy Schmidt at the famous "*ONE EYED JACK*" cabaret in Tokyo on February 27th, 2004. The cover design was created by Kien Tseng.

MOST SPECIAL ACKNOWLEDGEMENT

This book is dedicated to my lovely wife Machiko.

How do I love thee?

Let me count the ways: 'Just too many.'

Introduction

I first met Richard Roa in the fall of 1989. I was in the middle of researching *Tokyo Underworld* and someone had suggested I interview him because he knew the main character of the book, Nick Zapetti, and also because he worked for a time as a consultant to the *Toa-Sogo Kigyo*, a real-estate/leisure outfit based in Roppongi, which was, in fact, a transmogrification of the infamous Tokyo gang, the *Tosei-kai*, a yakuza organization which occupied another major part of the book.

My scheduled two-hour interview with Rick Roa metastasized into several lengthy Q&A session because the stories this man had to tell were so damned interesting, starting with the chilling tale he told of being caught in a Tokyo mob run clip joint and what he had to do to get his money back.

There was more—his hilarious tale of the American Train venture, his experiences as a bartender in the Ginza's most exclusive (and expensive) hostess club, his adventures with Bobby Brown and Whitney Houston in Japan. But, unfortunately, I could not use much of the material because it did not impact directly on the central thesis of Underworld, which dealt with the corrupt side of the U.S.-Japan relationship. But I always thought that it would make a good book one day, and lo and behold, here it is.

Rick Roa and I have become good friends over the years since those early interviews, and so it pleases me greatly to be able to write this introduction. I'm sure readers will enjoy this work as much as I did.

Robert Whiting,
Kamakura, 2004

1

A Trip Down Memory Lane...

Far better it is to dare mighty things, to win glorious triumphs, even though checkered by failure, than to take rank with those poor spirits who neither enjoy much nor suffer much, because they live in the gray twilight that knows not victory nor defeat.

—Theodore Roosevelt

Writing an autobiography is like being on sodium pentothal. You want to sit down and spill the beans on your life story. You imagine yourself talking across the bar to a group of sexy women—or maybe to a few young guys interested in knowing how you got stuck in Japan. People want to know how come I know so many celebrities both in Japan and the US. When people realize exactly who I am they ask questions like, "How did you get into that 'Tokyo Underworld' book? Isn't that a book about mobsters? Were you really friends with the book's main character Nick Zapetti?" Others ask, "Were you really a Playboy Japan director? How did you become the Kano Sisters' manager? Are they really sisters? Can you tell us their secrets?"

I've been asked a lot of questions about my life and work.

Someone once told me that the only stupid questions were the ones not asked.

Other people reminded me that if I told *my* whole life story that I would do a disappearing act.

Hey, you gotta die sometime!

I've worked with stars like Whitney Houston, Bobby Brown and icons like Dick Clark. I don't know if you've read the press on people like Whitney and other celebrities, but I can tell you: working with these kinds of people requires a certain finesse.

Working in Japan with Japanese business people and celebrities requires its own brand of finesse, and a finely-tuned understanding of Japan. I know Tokyo and have worked as a professional entrepreneur here for many years. I've also worked in its seedy and glitzy nightlife. I've done a lot of deals in the Tokyo town called Roppongi. This town is a mixture of rich ex-pats and business people along with thousands of hostesses.

The town of Roppongi is an accident waiting to happen.

During interviews for this book I spoke a lot about Roppongi. One of the many people helping me with the book liked my stories on Roppongi so much that he wanted to call me the "King of the Roppongi". He hasn't even been to Roppongi or even Japan but I plan to buy him a ticket. You never really know a place unless you've lived there. I've lived in Japan for over thirty-five years.

So back to my biography, first you start to think…and you remember…and you talk to friends…and you find people who jar more memories. The memories don't always fit together perfectly, so you have to figure out where the other pieces are. Before you know it you're sitting there with a half-done jigsaw puzzle, and you know there's nothing to do but keep fitting the damn pieces in until it's finished.

I've done a lot of crazy things and been to a lot of screwed up places in my lifetime.

I've had people try to kill me.

I've had successes (not getting killed is one), and I've made stupid mistakes (you'll hear about those escapades in later chapters). Putting it all in a book is something I've wanted to do for a long time. I wanted to tell anyone who might be interested what it's like to be born in Brooklyn, New York, an American icon city, in the most powerful country in the world, and then travel to a country still recovering from abject poverty and devastating defeat in war. I watched Japan grow into an economic powerhouse, second only to the behemoth American economy. I wanted to say how sweet it's been to be a part of the relationship between those two great countries, the United States and Japan. I've been lucky enough to spend most of my adult life in Japan, where I've seen a country nation build itself up into a huge economic power. I've watched Tokyo go from holes in the ground to towering skyscrapers.

And I didn't just sit on my ass and watch. I created part of that town, and I had lots of fun doing it!

I took another trip down memory lane about a dozen years ago. It was a trip that occurred well into the story I'm about to tell, but it's a chapter that might fit best here, at the beginning. It happened in February 1991, before I'd ever heard of Harrow School, or the Kano Sisters, or Bill Clinton. But I had already spearheaded The Great American Train, and I'd worked with Dick Clark, and I'd watched Nick Zapetti live and die. I had a two-decade old marriage that had not gone well, except for one thing: my son, Justin.

Justin and I were going to America. It was his first time. Not only that, but the Tokyo Broadcasting Station was going to send a camera crew along. They would film our every move, through airports, car rides, and walks by the river. The idea of an American father taking his Japanese son on a tour of their American roots fit perfectly with a program TBS was producing. The program cast a wide net as it explored the complex relationship between the two cultures. It probed into the background of war, and the hard-earned peace. It recalled the sacrifices of both sides. It looked at the poverty from which Japan's postwar boom grew. It also gave a snapshot of a failing American city: Detroit, which had lost so much of its automobile industry, and had sunk to its lowest ebb in 1991 (by the way, Japan was kicking our ass in that industry but we Americans can learn quick, and we did—now Detroit is in top form—Go America!)

The program also showed the growing links and harmony between the two countries. Here was an American learning Japanese music theory. Here were old soldiers—one-time enemies who now could see each other as friends. Finally, the camera focused on an American, who'd settled in Japan in the midst of all that history, taking his twenty-year-old son to see the people and places of his boyhood. Wow, was I a proud father.

My family still lived on the East Coast, and because of that distance, and the fact that I'd visited New York from time to time, they had never come to Japan. With less than 20% of Americans owning passports it's typical that folks do not travel to foreign countries much. When I first came to Japan the only foreign countries American civilians traveled to regularly were Mexico and Canada. Even among travel-minded Americans, those who live on the East Coast went to Europe, and my own family—being Spanish speakers—would have been more likely to go to Mexico. The Pacific is just too wide an expanse for those who aren't used to it. They depended on me to tell them about exotic Japan on my visits home.

Even today the American passport rate is low. My fellow Americans should go out and visit this fantastic country of Japan. Anyone who's owned a Japanese product should come and meet the people who make these things. But don't all come at once, I still want my seat at the best restaurants!

I'd visited the States sporadically up to 1991. There was a stretch of eight years when I didn't go at all, but then there had been periods when I crossed the Pacific a couple of times a month. I was always happy to go back because everyone was interested in seeing me. They all would ask me: "Rick, what's going on in Japan? What makes you want to stay there?" I would tell them about the opportunity, the great people, the Roppongi women, and the beauty of Mount Fuji. I would describe odd customs, and the different way of doing business. They were fascinated by all those things, but what I liked to tell them about the most was my son, and of course, he was what my family wanted to hear about.

It was a special time. As I told the TBS interviewer on camera, it was important that Justin experience those things at that moment. Before then he might have been too young to truly appreciate it. A child is too absorbed in himself to have time to learn about the great differences in the world. Later Justin would enter the world of business. While that's a wonderful world, it also has its narrowness and tunnel-vision. At twenty he was suspended between youth, and being grown up. He was at that stage where a young man wants to see everything at once. I wanted him to see America through family—through people who had a real, blood connection with him. In that way he could appreciate that part of the wider world.

Twenty—it's a moment like no other.

When TBS edited their footage into a TV program they began our portion by showing clips of the life we were leaving in Tokyo. There was Justin having fun with his friends, just like any young man anywhere. Here was his Dad on the subway, and striding through the Tokyo streets. There was even a drink at the end of the day in a softly lit bar.

At one point in the program they showed photographs of Justin, his mother, and me. Then there he was in his Little League uniform. He was an awfully good baseball player. I explained that a part of my adaptation to Japanese culture had come in accepting my wife's methods of raising our boy. I had my influence, and I always provided for them, but Justin, being born in Japan, would be more Japanese. I told how I had come to accept this as the right thing to do for my son. Hey, we were living in Japan!

But Justin's mother hadn't kept me from showing my son some aspects of an American's approach to life. His father was a maverick among the Japanese, and Justin knew it. Now he would see the root source of that.

I think one of the biggest kicks Justin got on the trip was when he went to a Raiders football game, and was surrounded by beautiful cheerleaders. When I looked at him in the middle of all those pretty faces, I knew that was my boy.

But the most meaningful part of the trip was in New York. We arrived at the airport, and there were the relatives: his grandfather, aunts, uncles, cousins—Justin was pretty overwhelmed, but that didn't keep him from charming all of them. His grandfather said to me: "You did good."

Later the camera crew recorded a dinner for everyone. We had it at a hotel on Long Island. Justin was the guest of honor, and he spoke what little English he knew. I got him up before everyone, and he said loud and clear: "I'm so happy to see everyone." They gave him a round of applause. Before the evening was out he was singing with his cousins.

But there was another moment worth noting. The footage begins with me sitting in a van. "Right at home," I say. "Yeah, I remember it. I know these streets. Eastern Parkway…" We were rolling through my old neighborhood: Brooklyn. We went to my old address. The house was still there, and the neighborhood was more or less intact. There were changes, of course. There were more black people, and less Italians, but that was just a matter of proportions. It was still the streets I'd grown up in.

A black man came up the steps, and I realized he was the guy from the fruit cart. "You still stealing bananas, Rick?"

"Hey, I never stole any bananas," I quipped, and we both laughed. I asked him if he was still selling fruit.

"Naw, man, I'm a licensed electrician now," he said. "Is this your boy?"

"This is Justin."

He looked him over. "Justin, just don't you steal any bananas. And you get a good education, you hear?"

People—they are the same everywhere; the same, yet different, which is what makes life so sweet. I realized that as we went down into the street, and pitched pennies, just as we had when I was a kid. I was a little rusty at it, just as I was a little rusty at this memory business. But as enough people asked enough questions, and the audience gathered round the bar, I found myself recalling all kinds of things….

2

Brooklyn—A Boy of the Streets

My parents were very Old World. They come from Brooklyn, which is the heart of the Old World. Their values in life are God and carpeting.

—Woody Allen

I was born in Brooklyn, New York, which at one time was counted as the third largest city in the US. Brooklyn had the first African-American major league baseball player, Jackie Robinson, and boy could he play. When the Brooklyn Dodgers left town in 57' we mourned for years. Truman Capote wrote *Breakfast at Tiffany's* in a Brooklyn flat. We had (and still have) the Brooklyn Bridge, which took 14 years and 27 lives to build. It's been offered for sale a million times, but in truth Brooklyn would never give it up.

In the '30s and '40s Brooklyn was a melting pot of immigrants trying to make a buck. The Borough included Italians, Jews, Poles and Irishmen, with more minorities amongst the minorities. Among these latter folks were my relatives from Spain. This immigrant soup made the town famous and infamous throughout the world. Scorsese in *Goodfellas* and Spike Lee in many of his films are just two examples of Brooklyn's place in America's cultural clambake. *Goodfellas* best represents the Brooklyn I knew. When I saw that movie I thought I was looking through a time window.

Brooklyn was the shit back then. Along with our Dodgers, we had the gangs, and the quintessential American life: immigrants trying to make it. Woody Allen, Barbara Streisand and Cyndi Lauper came out

7

of that. Mike Tyson got his start there. Brooklyn breeds a killer instinct that if used correctly makes champions. If abused, that instinct makes people self-destruct. I've seen both. So has Mike Tyson.

After immigrating to America my dad, Rudolph Roa put down roots in Brooklyn. He and three of his bothers had emigrated from Spain and originally went to Columbia. It was the 1930s, and Spain was very unsettled at the time. Whether they fled the Civil War is something I've never known. Once they got to Cali, Columbia in South America they found they didn't like it there either. My relatives were artisans working in jewelry and metalworking; most folks in Cali grew specialized plants. It wasn't a good fit. The three brothers Rudolf, Ascanio and Frederick packed their bags and left for New York. It was a typical immigrant story. Once you left home you stayed in motion until you found a place that you could take, and that would take you. If you didn't like one place you went to the next. I guess my dad liked Brooklyn.

My dad met my mother in New York. Her name was Helen, and she was living at home with my grandmother and grandfather. They were immigrants, having come here from England a few years before. Over there they'd lived in London. Over here they settled in Brooklyn, and that was where Mom moved in with Dad. Mom was only about 21 or 22 when she married Dad.

She had me first, then came my brother, Bayardo. Bayardo chose the dark side. He would always have problems and I think this had something to do with him moving out of Brooklyn. Maybe his troubles were inevitable because of the start he had. Who knows? When we were just babies, my father left, separating from my mom, and he took Bayardo with him. My mother kept me and we lived in Brooklyn. My father took my brother to Columbia to live with my father's parents. As a result my brother and I had totally different childhoods in every way. We were from different cultures. I was brought up in the English atmosphere in my grandparents' house, while my brother was brought up in a strictly Spanish way.

I don't remember my English grandfather very well. He died when I was a little kid. I never even met my Spanish grandfather. He was rumored to own an orchid plantation in Cali. My English grandmother is another story. She tried her best to bring me up. When I was 12 years old my mother died of cancer. Since my dad was gone, and there was no one else to take me, my grandmother took over the job. There wasn't much she could do at that point. It was a time and place where a kid wanted to be out on his own by the time he was 11 or 12. I was uncontrollable without even trying. Once I was out the front door it just happened. Brooklyn took a ten-year-old boy and turned him into a man by twelve, if he didn't get killed or arrested first.

I'd found my niche, and I was sticking to it. I was a boy of the streets. My grandmother and I lived in the Bedford-Stuyvesant section, a tough area in a city full of tough areas. I grew up on the streets. It was an Italian neighborhood with all the little Italian joints, and the guys on the street corners, and the vegetable stands—the whole thing. There were Italians who'd come from the boot, Naples, Rome, and so on, then there were the Sicilians. We had plenty of those. The sections were like that then: the Italians in this neighborhood and the Jews in that neighborhood, and Polacks over there, and blacks over here, so we all had our turf. We were around Eastern Parkway in East New York. There was no question about power in our neighborhood: the guineas ruled.

As life moved along in New York I assumed my father and brother were living in Cali. As far as I knew my father and my brother were there with my father's brothers. But that was easy to forget. It wasn't as if they wrote us. They'd disappeared from our lives long before my mother had died. I never missed them at all.

Once when I was six or seven my father's mother came to New York along with my brother, Bayardo. I'm not sure I'd ever been aware that I'd had a brother, and they didn't want me to know. They introduced us as cousins. We were just little kids, and we fooled around together the way little kids do.

It was awkward for the grownups—it didn't last. Pretty soon my grandmother and "Cousin" Bayardo went back to Columbia. A few years later Mom passed away from cancer. I was only twelve. That left me to grow up in the streets with the gangs.

The gangs seemed to be the only way to go. My only other choice was my grandmother's apartment, and that wasn't much fun. It wasn't horrible. There just wasn't any excitement. Out in the street we had our gangs—our boys, you know. We belonged. I think that's a basic urge in life, especially with a kid. When you're just starting out in the world you want to belong. You may be destined to become a maverick in some other time or place, but when you're 12 you only want to be hanging around with ten other guys—part of a gang. We had our rituals and rules, and we had our area. Every day after school we'd go there, and it really was ours.

Not that there weren't other things. There was school. Somehow I made time for that for a while. I started out going to school at P.S. 137 in Bedford-Stuyvesant. I used to pitch pennies for cigarettes. I went to Junior High 73. By the time I was 16 or 17 we were living in this cold water flat at 276 Sumter Street. We'd have block parties there. We had lots of cockroaches, big ones and small ones, and we had a mouse. There were bedbugs. You don't hear much about bedbugs anymore except in nursery rhymes, but we had armies of them in New York, and I think a lot of them were stationed in my bed. We didn't think too much about it. Stuff like that would be a big deal now, but it wasn't back then.

What was it like with my gang? It was a life that just isn't there today. It was great! Today you hear about nothing but murder, and drug dealing with gangs. We got into mischief, but nothing like that. In our own neighborhood my friends and I hung out wherever we wanted. Outside our own turf we were more careful. We walked the streets, and we had a sort of clubhouse down in the basement of this building that wasn't being used for anything. We called ourselves the Top Hats. We had jackets each with a picture of a top hat on the back.

We all had big pompadours with DAs. DA stands for "Duck's Ass." It's when you grow your hair a little long in the back and comb it back and out, like a Duck's Ass. That was the popular style in Brooklyn in the late '40's and '50s. We were twenty years ahead of our time. This was the '50s, but if you watch John Travolta and his gang in *Saturday Night Fever* you're watching a Hollywood version of us.

We strutted around, did a lot of dancing. We weren't quite as old as the guys in Travolta's movie, but when I saw it two decades later I still felt like I was watching myself. Most of the guys I knew were Sicilians. A lot of their fathers and older brothers were connected—soldiers in the gangs. They were the real thing: mobsters. They were the kind of guys who didn't have to show they were tough. Everybody knew it. Not having parents of my own, I ate at their houses, so I grew up on Italian food: lasagna, pasta, and red wine made down in the cellar. In most of these houses grandma and grandpa couldn't speak English, and even some of my friends' mothers and fathers only spoke broken English.

Out on the streets we pitched pennies, and made out with the girls. Of course we were only thirteen or fourteen years old, but we were pretty macho. We didn't know what we were doing, but we did it anyway. At thirteen I learned to play pool. We used to play at the pool hall down on Halsey Street and Broadway. Times were good.

I grew up, and lost contact with those guys over the years. I don't really hear anything of them anymore, though some years later I did hear something about my best buddy, Al Henney. His father was a Seven-Day Adventist. I heard Al became a professor up in Connecticut. But that was the last I ever heard of any of them. Some of them probably stayed right there, while others moved, and I went off to the other side of the world.

When I went back to visit my hometown recently I found it interesting to see how things had changed. Change is the one constant in this world. I recently checked out our old apartment. My grandmother and I lived in something like a slum, at least that's what a lot of people would've called it. But today they might not call that building a slum. Today those same people who looked down on it would spend a pile of money just for the chance to fix it up. It was one of those beautiful brownstone buildings that they renovate now, calling them "treasures of yesteryear." Back then they were just beat-up old buildings. We were poor and didn't have much, but it had always been that way. I wanted more, but I didn't get obsessed with it. Mostly I just wanted to have fun.

In the years since my father had gone away we'd heard nothing at all about him. An incredibly fat lady lived down on the first floor. She was the only person in the building who had a telephone. One day she got a call that had a lot to do with my life. The only problem was: she didn't tell me.

That call came from a girl named Olga. I don't know how Olga had found out about me. Maybe someone had let something slip about a boy here in Brooklyn. But Olga, my dad's daughter, and my half-sister had hunted me down. I didn't know that my dad had a new woman in his life. I knew nothing of a daughter either. She learned the phone number of my building, and called it. That meant she called the fat lady. The fat lady told her: yes, your half brother lives here. So a few days later this girl appeared at the building. She was about 14, and she was with my dark-side brother, Bayardo. She said: "I'm your half-sister, Olga, and this is your brother, Bayardo." They stood there looking at me with smiles. I was shocked.

I had no idea what to do with these two, how to treat them or feel about them. I had nothing in common with them. I'd never seen Olga, and though I had met my brother I'd always thought he was my cousin.

Talk about screwed up American families. There I was, 16 years old, already needing Tony Soprano's psychiatrist!

But I had to deal with this. There they were. Suddenly I'd lost a cousin, while gaining a brother and a half sister. I wasn't sure how to deal with all this family stuff. For years I'd had a grandmother who didn't bother me, and nothing more. I was free. I was running my own life. I had my guys, my boys, my gang, playing pool, and now all of a sudden these two showed up. I said: "You're who?"

My immediate reaction was to turn away. I didn't cut them off, but I stepped back a little. It was instinct. I couldn't jump into something I didn't know about. Gradually I got used to keeping in touch with Olga, but my brother went from bad to real bad. There was nothing I could do about that, and I didn't try very hard. Even at that age he was getting into things he shouldn't. He went from dope to robbing drug stores. He was on his way to a sad life. But my half-sister was good. She told me where my father was.

My dad, Rudolph had returned to New York, married a Puerto Rican woman, and they were living in downtown Brooklyn. He owned a grocery store. But his wife was insanely jealous, and that jealousy was aimed at any and all of us in his old family. She didn't want to have anything to do with me. It was one of those things.

But the daughter, my half-sister, Olga kept calling me now and then. My brother wandered off, seeming to vanish into thin air. This would happen again and again for decades. There were also my father's two brothers. These were the two who'd been down in Columbia all these years. Now they were in New York. They'd married Italian women, and whenever I saw them they were very good to me.

So I did my growing up on the street with a family that seemed to shift around me without much rhyme or reason. With my father leaving and my mom dying I had to learn fast. I did. I grew up faster than a kid should, but I don't think it hurt me. It taught me how to think on my feet. I learned that things can change completely at the drop of a hat, maybe a Top Hat. There are worse things to learn. As I got into my late teens I wasn't sure what I was going to do with myself, but events took care of that. The Army had a uniform with my name on it. I didn't mind going. What else was I going to do?

While I was in basic training, my half-sister got married. Eventually she had four sons. One of those boys is now Assistant District Attorney of New York. I went into the service, and there I learned more about how to live in the grownup world. It wasn't the street, but there were things that were the same. It was a bunch of guys all thrown together in a platoon, and it wasn't so different than a bunch of guys on the street. But it was more organized, and it had a real purpose. That was different, and I noticed it. Still, there in all that discipline I began to realize what a maverick I was, and it dawned on me that I wasn't exactly like everybody else. I could have fun, and I could get in trouble. And I wasn't always ready to stand at attention. There was just too much of me that wanted to have fun. Too much of anything is no good.

I had so much fun I got court-martialed for it. It was one of those things. I was a little tipsy…or was it just plain drunk? There was our colonel's jeep, and I needed a car. You know how alcohol can cut down on inhibitions a little? Anyway, I had a definite need of a joy ride—straight to my girlfriend's house. Well, maybe not straight. When I came back in the morning, everyone noticed the bent fenders. So I got a summary court-martial, and was fined 25 dollars. I lost a stripe, but got it back a few months later

Maybe I'd had too much fun. Maybe the army hadn't taught me enough. These were some of the thoughts in my mind as I got out. I'd done my time. Now I was home, and I wasn't sure what to do. I went to live in Oradell in Bergen County New Jersey, with my grandmother's sister, my Aunt Mary and Uncle John. After my wild man antics in the service, I had this idea of living in Jersey and straightening up. I thought it would help me to get my life in order. I drove a taxi for a while, trying to go back to school. I joined a theatre guild, and became a—well, a sort of funny actor. The town I was living in was Oradell, just over the George Washington Bridge. They had the Oradell Playhouse. My biggest reason for joining their acting troupe was that they had a lot of good-looking women. That's what started it, but it wasn't long before I had a real interest in acting. It would never be first on my list, but it was interesting, and I began to appreciate the skills involved. I wound up doing three or four plays. I was a good looking guy when I was younger. I was kind of rough and tough, which wasn't what they were used to dealing with in those placid Jersey suburbs, so there should have been some parts that were right for me. My problem was that I was altogether new to this, and though I was learning, I wasn't very good at it. That would take time, and at the age of 24 I was impatient.

Instead of acting I took up stage managing. The job had benefits. The women loved the stage manager. I must have screwed every actress there. It was like Disneyland. I thought this situation was unique until I arrived in Asia years later. I enjoyed that too, and I was a much better stage manager than I was an actor!

But I was destined for other things, and I knew it. I didn't know where I was going, but I was sure I was going to find something, and whatever it was, it would bring both money and a lot of fun. I wanted to go overseas. Those were my dreams.

All of those dreams would come true, but it took a little doing.

3

Across the Ocean

My trip to Asia begins here in Japan for an important reason. It begins here because for a century and a half now, America and Japan have formed one of the great and enduring alliances of modern times. From that alliance has come an era of peace in the Pacific.

—**George W. Bush** Tokyo, Feb. 18, 2002

(I think our recent Commander in Chief apparently forgot about a little something called World War II. Maybe he should have spoken to his father.)

I got first my taste of living overseas in the Army when I did a hitch in Korea. I'd been drafted. It happened to just about every guy back then. It was the Cold War, and America had bases all over, trying to wall in the commies. We had troops in Europe, Asia, and everywhere in between. I became one of those GIs, and some say I must have had my head screwed on backwards because I liked it.

Korean life for the GI, if you call being in war a life, suited me just fine. We were in a goddamn war but there were cultural benefits. Some of my comrades who went back to the states would talk about Korean culture. The only culture I liked when I was twenty was getting laid every week with a different gorgeous girl.

Even today in Tokyo I see young hotshot bankers and stock traders from places like New York and London. Many of them never want to go back home. Many say they like the culture of the place. Even at my age, I understand.

I'd grown up in the Big Apple, and as cosmopolitan as that city is, I knew it wasn't the whole world. Japan was a place that was totally different in culture, geography, and everything else. I'd only dreamed of such places. I wanted to see more—and the girls—what a great culture!

So, I did my time, caused my trouble, came home, and if I'd been a normal GI that would've been about it.

If I'd followed the normal GI story line I would've worked some job, married some girl, raised some kids, and though I probably would've done all right by myself, I never would have explored the world. I couldn't do those things in the normal stateside way. I wasn't a kid in a street gang anymore. I was slowly discovering that I was a true maverick.

One of the first real jobs I had after I got out of the Army was as a store detective. I'd already been working, but it was all odd jobs with odd hours. I had the goal of working overseas again but instead I was driving a taxi in Jersey—I drove one of Bill Lathan's four cars.

Bill was a short, fat guy with greased slicked back hair. He was married to an obnoxious and unforgiving woman. "If I ever catch you guys stealing I'll cut your balls off," she used to say. I remember old Bill saying, "If you can't steal any money driving for me you shouldn't be working for me."

Our dispatcher would slur driving instructions, probably from drinking on the job. His instructions were usually wrong. At times I felt as if I were driving my life down a road with no direction. Was it the instructions? The road? Or the life?

I seemed farther from my aims than ever. Don't we all sometimes?

I'd learned even at that age that the only thing you got from sitting on your ass was old. And if you were in the US Army and you sat on your ass you'd probably take a bullet. I decided to make a change and get a better job.

One day I saw an interesting ad in the newspaper from a company called E.J. Korvette's in Paramus. They were looking for a store detective. I went over there, and got interviewed by a man named Jim Markley. He was a sturdy guy, about 5' 7" with gray hair. He looked like a bank president, but it turned out he was a retired 1st grade detective out of New York. Jim was a truly tough guy—he'd earned the label solving crimes across the river. He looked at me, and with his practiced eye he could see I was off the streets. He asked me where I was from. I said Brooklyn.

He asked, "You ever been arrested?"

"No," I said.

"Oh, really?" he asked. "Are you sure you've never been arrested?"

I said, "Yeah."

"Can I run a check on you?" he asked.

I said, "Sure."

He said, "Really? You're pretty street smart, aren't you?"

I said, "Of course." Tough or not, I wasn't worried about him. I knew he wouldn't find anything on me. I'd gotten my stripe back in the army, and my civilian record was clean.

It was about a week later when the phone rang. It was Jim M. for me. He said, "Come in here. I'm going to hire you. You've seen enough, and know enough, so you'll make a good detective." So he took me under his wing, and I became one of the best store detectives E.J. Korvette's ever had. Like he'd said, I was street smart. I knew what to watch for, and what to do.

Now I had a real job, but it wasn't what I'd wanted. I knew that from the start, and Jim knew it too. I never held back from him that my real dream was to go overseas again. But he would say: "There's plenty to do right here, Rick. This can turn into a very good job for you." I'd listen, but I didn't believe it. The maverick in me was already on the move.

The Sunday New York Times had this overseas job section: little boxes with dreams in them. Every week I would look at those boxes, trying to find one that was gift-wrapped for me. There must be something I was qualified to do somewhere else in the world. They needed teachers, translators—all kinds of things—but I couldn't find one that fit my skills. Then I heard that ITT was looking for trainees in electronics. They needed somebody to do quality control and stock management, and the jobs were all overseas. They had a subsidiary company: Automated Electric. The work would be with them.

This wasn't too far a stretch from work I'd done in the service. I called and scheduled an interview. I dressed for it, and was ready to impress whoever was on the other side of that desk. The interviewer turned out to be a guy a good bit older than me. I figured out right away that he too was a Korean veteran. He'd been there when the fighting was still going on. He'd retired as a colonel. He asked me if I'd been in the service, and I said I had. I mentioned that I'd been to Korea.

At that moment I knew I'd said the right thing. I could smell something good coming. I put myself back into the full army headset. Every time the Colonel said something to me I said: "Yessir." Colonels tend to like that response. I didn't let up. I showed him I could do that yes-sir-no-sir stuff with the best of them. I practically "sirred" him to death.

This colonel was no different. It was the kind of thing he was used to, so I was just making him comfortable. As I got up to leave, he said: "We're going to seriously consider you."

"Yessir!" I said, snapping to attention.

The Colonel knew he had what he needed.

After the interview I went back to E.J. Korvette's, and there I found Jim.

I said: "Jim, I had a great interview today."

"Really?" he asked. I could tell he wasn't entirely happy about that.

"Yeah," I said. "It's overseas stuff, and the guy seemed to like how I handled myself. Maybe I'll get something here."

Right then Jim said to me: "Rick, I'm going to be transferred to New York. I'm going to be chief of security for all of Korvette's on the East Coast."

"That's great," I told him.

Then he said: "But I want you to come with me. I'll make you my assistant."

It was a good offer, but I already knew what my reply had to be. "I'll be honest with you, Jim," I said. "I've told you all along, I was going for something overseas, so I've got to go for this other thing. It's my first choice. But if it doesn't work, I'll consider it."

Korvette's—even a Korvette's top job in New York—was tempting, but it wasn't my goal. My goal was to see the world, and at that moment it was within my reach.

About a week later the Colonel called me up, and said: "We'd like to have you."

I didn't think about it. I just said: "Yes."

"Ok. There are two assignments: Would you like to go to Europe? Or would you like to go to the Bahamas." I was stunned. Here I was, stuck in an E.J. Korvette's in Paramus, New Jersey, and now, suddenly I had my choice of exotic assignments: two places I'd never been near before. Then I thought about the choice I'd been given, and I said: "Sir, *I'd* pay *you* to let me go to the Bahamas."

Luckily I didn't have to pay him. It was the other way around, and the pay wasn't bad. I arrived in the Bahamas with a job and a regular paycheck, and I saw how good another part of the world could be. If it wasn't perfect, the weather was certainly better than Brooklyn's, or Korea's for that matter. It was warm, sunny, and there were beautiful women there too. (And I'd thought Korea was Disneyland!)

That's how it started, and I've been overseas ever since.

I was in the Bahamas for a little over a year. I learned a lot, and came out of there as a quality control engineer. At that time they were putting in the Underwater Test and Evaluation Command. Our job was to build a range where they would test nuclear-powered subs and their missiles. The range was off Andros Island. It was a workplace that was not too far at all from the playground. What kid could want more?

I was continually amazed at how easy it had been. There I'd been in this concrete city up north, then all a sudden I'm plopped down right in the middle of the Bahamas. I loved the water, and I was in heaven. I had a job where I could learn skills that would guarantee me these kinds of jobs long into the future. I liked the people I worked with, including my boss, Andy Moe.

Andy Moe and I got to be pretty good friends. He was a vet too, and we got drunk together now and then. We liked the same things: drinking, women, and having a good time. Nassau was and is still an incredible town for a young single man. Every day tour boats from the States would pull into port. These boats were full of young single ladies with nothing particular to do with themselves. We made ourselves very available to them. In a town like that people don't act the way they do at home. Women in that situation are always ready for their vacation fling. We were there to give it to them.

It was with great regret that I finished that job. Nassau is a place of many fond memories. I think we all wondered why we hadn't made it go on longer. But we were pros, and not the kind to drag our feet just for pleasure. There would be plenty more where this came from. The job had lasted a year. I'd gotten the work I'd wanted off the shores of the United States. I'd had a taste, and it left me wanting more.

Before I'd left the Bahamas Andy had told me: "Rick, you look me up when you get back to Paramus. I'll already be up there. I'll have a temporary office and I want you to visit me there. Do it quick. I won't be there long. I'm going to be reassigned to Europe, so if you want to come to Europe with me, we'll do it." My answer to that was easy: "Great." So even before I went home I knew I had a way out again. It was exactly what I wanted.

When I got up to New Jersey I'd barely unpacked my suitcase before I went to his office. When I walked in the people called me: "Mr. Roa." I thought: I'm certainly coming up in the world. I'm 'Mr.' Roa now." They told me how to get to Andy Moe's office. I went to his door, and found him working.

"Hi, Andy," I said, "I'm here."

He looked up from what he was doing. He wasn't surprised. "Rick, I'm happy to see you," he said. "Will you be ready to leave for Germany in a week?"

I shrugged, and said: "Of course. Why wouldn't I be?"

"Good. Then plan on it. I'll go first and get everything set up. Your tickets will be ready for you."

A week later I was in Wiesbaden in West Germany. I had a great time there. It was still the postwar era. The Germans were glad to have Americans around. Sure, we'd beaten them in war, but they respected that, and now we were doing the right thing, defending them against the Russian bear, and helping them get as rich as we were. The Germans could see that, but the French didn't always agree.

I traveled all over Europe while I was there. It was about the time the French threw our forces out of their country. The U.S. had important radar installations in France, so when we left the Air Force had to reposition all its radar. Once again I was the quality control guy on a defense project. Work and play took me to a lot of different countries. It was an education—my education. I had to have a secret clearance. Even with that (or maybe especially with that) I couldn't go to any of the Eastern Bloc countries. Still, I had a great time. I was living my dream. What I didn't know was how that dream would expand. It expanded years later more than I could ever imagine.

4

To the Land of the Rising Sun

Nations do not mistrust each other because they are armed, they are armed because they mistrust each other.

—Ronald Reagan, 1986

It was 1967 when my company ran out of European projects. At the time about five hundred of us were working on various technical contracts for the American military machine. It was one of the iciest periods of the Cold War, and there hadn't been so much as a hint of a thaw since Vietnam had heated up a couple of years before. All you needed to do was watch the napalm on the evening news to know the world was on fire. The United States was trying to contain Russia and vice versa. Paranoia was fueling the flames of the war machine and I was a cog in that engine.

Increases in military funds went anywhere a system had to be installed or upgraded. We were ringing in the communist nations with submarines, naval bases, air bases, and even ground troops. Today it's hard to believe the size of this mammoth operation. Although in most parts of the world no bullets were flying, it was one of the most extensive wars in history. We covered the whole fucking planet with bases and operations. Your tax dollars at work!

Eventually the West won the Cold War with good old private enterprise. That's what I was part of when I first came to Japan. The way it worked was this: the larger defense-oriented companies would bid for military contracts worldwide. When a company got one it would look for the right contractors to do the work. Some of these contractors were little companies—guys with just a few people working. Others were individuals like me. They had a list of what people and companies could do what work. I was on the list, and any interested company could find me. I was a freelancer for my country.

That year GTE found me. They hired me to go to work for one of their subsidiaries, Automated Electric Company out of Chicago. Automated Electric had a GTE defense contract to install the Automatic Voice Network at various bases in the Far East. It was one more cog in the U.S. war machine along the Pacific Rim. From the Aleutians to Australia the U.S. was conducting surveillance, intercepting radio traffic, and keeping its own military ready. Our own company had people doing this in Japan, Guam, Taiwan, and at Clark Air Base in the Philippines. They sent me to the Philippines.

As I mentioned earlier, I'd been in the Far East before, back when I'd served my Army hitch in Korea. That had been my first taste of foreign life, and I'd liked it. Now I was back, but in a very different place. The Philippines was down in the tropics well to the south of Korea. It had been an American possession for a half a century, then had gained independence after World War II. Before the war General Douglas McArthur had been in the Philippines for several years, helping those people form an army in preparation for independence. The war had interrupted that. What little military they had crumbled alongside the Americans. During the war the Philippines was the place where General McArthur had famously vowed: "I will return." He'd said it, then sailed to Australia, leaving the islands to the invaders, but less than three years later he'd made good on his promise.

I stayed at McArthur's old headquarters, a place call Dau. It had beautiful big wooden, white buildings. Most of us there were civilians working on defense-oriented contracts. We were not far from the air base. Clark Air Base was a stop for soldiers and supplies going to Vietnam. We saw a lot of American boys coming and going. The GIs came up there for R&R.

Not far outside Clark was a place called Angeles City. If you ask any old army or navy guy about the Sin City of the Pacific Rim during those decades, he'll figure you're asking about that place. Angeles City was the epitome of fun, vice and crazy degeneracy. You could get anything you wanted there. I can't even begin to tell you what we did. Hell, I probably couldn't even remember all of it. Sex came in all shapes and sizes. Clubs came in all shapes and sizes. It was like being in the most bizarre, wide-ranging international restaurant in the world, a place where you could give your waiter the most complicated, impossible order, and he'd come back with it in twenty minutes. In the meantime you'd sip a drink that had god-knows-what in it, and be propositioned a dozen times.

Prostitution was the main activity. The clubs, the restaurants, and every other part of the Angeles City economy revolved around the prostitutes. There were too many of them to count. Most were Filipino, but to hear them talk you'd figure you were in an international bazaar. These girls' immediate goal was to get money. Some of it went to their pimps, some to clothes, jewelry, and make-up, and when they could they sent money home to their families. It didn't take many American dollars to make life a whole lot easier for a Filipino family. But while that was a girl's day-to-day goal, the ultimate prize was to marry an American serviceman. A lot of them did. Plenty of American boys found the attentions these girls gave them were what they had always wanted, and the girls knew that even the slim American military paycheck went a *long* way in the Philippines. The girls would live off base, but on payday they'd all go shopping on the base in the PX and commissary. They'd buy tons and tons of food, most of which would wind up in the stores off base.

If you were a bachelor, making money—which I was—the world was your oyster there. I was young, single and had no real reason to think past tomorrow. I got a paycheck considerably bigger than that of most of the American servicemen. I was also playing poker, and I was playing it well. Between the exotic women, and poker winnings, I was enjoying myself immensely.

When my boss in Japan called me up and asked: ""How would you like to pull up stakes, and come up to Japan?" I replied: "I'd rather not." I didn't have to go into detail as to why. He knew where I was, and what held me there. Already knowing the arguments I would raise, he had a counter for each of them. Women? Japan had plenty, and they were as exotic as any I'd seen. "Beauty's in the culture," he said. "Haven't you ever heard of a geisha?" Along with a whole nation of beautiful women, there would be a fat salary increase. Poker winnings? How about some company stock as an ante? Then he pointed out that Tokyo wouldn't let me down for nightlife either. It was famous among GIs and officers alike as an R&R playground. I gave it some thought. I could keep on checking the quality of components in our fight against the commies, and continue winning poker hands at my Cold War outpost, or I could try my luck in a real world capital. It didn't take me long to decide.

I flew here from the Philippines on August 1st, 1968. As we came across Honshu, Japan's main island, we flew over the cone of Fuji. I watched steam and clouds floating around Fuji's snow-covered slopes. Mount Fuji is an incredible resting volcano with as well defined a cone as you'll ever see. She pops about once every four hundred and fifty years. Fuji is the nation's signature. As I saw it that first time I could almost smell it. There, I thought, is the incense of Japan.

They had somebody waiting for me at the airport to take me up to the air base. This was already the headquarters of the 15th Air Force. There we had a command site.

My job was to work on microwave towers. The telephone signals could travel by three routes: through microwave towers, satellites, and cables. I would have two telephones on my desk, and I would dial a coded number on one. The signal would go up through the microwave towers, then way up to the satellite, then round the world, and down into a cable, and then my other phone would ring a few seconds later.

That was the kind of stuff we were doing to check the systems and make sure they worked. Some of it was that simple, some was more complex, but it was vital to our opening up a lead in the technical race with the Russians.

The Japanese were our close allies. With energy and discipline they had recovered and rebuilt from the ashes of their defeat, and become the leading economy in Asia. They took in raw materials from outside, and sent it back out as cameras and cars. They had their own unique free enterprise system. This made them natural allies with us Americans. The Japanese believed and practiced Realpolitik. Right after the war Japan had begun producing small cars, radios, and other finished products in factories where the assembly lines were set out on dirt floors. American bombs had decimated their nation, and they had finally surrendered, but that didn't mean they'd given up. These people still knew they had it in them to build a great country. Twenty-three years after the War's end I arrived in time to see that comeback going into high gear. Japan had dug out from a mountain of debt by making and selling cheap cameras and radios to America and Europe. Now they had capital of their own, and they were ready for the jump into cars and computers.

I was fascinated by what I was seeing. One of the things I remember best from my first days here was walking around Tokyo, and everywhere I looked there was a hole. You turned a corner, and there was a hole, you topped a hill, and there was another. From a bird's eye view, it looked like Swiss cheese! They were building everywhere. The holes were like seeds being sown. Every hole meant new offices or apartments or stores. A whole new Tokyo was in the works.

I saw those holes, and I thought: this is pretty interesting. I'm going to have to stick around awhile, and see what happens. So I did. So far I've stuck around for three-and-a-half decades.

There were a lot of Americans living in Japan when I first got here. Many of them were military retirees. Some had fought in the war, while others had done hitches in that part of the world. They'd come to admire the culture and attitudes of Japan. I was about to join them in that admiration.

There were certain lines of separation. Many Americans spent most of their time with other Americans. We had our own cliques, and made our own friends. Many of the guys who'd arrived before I did already had businesses. They were established. We Americans were really doing our own wheeling and dealing.

There was plenty of interaction between American-owned businesses and Japanese-owned businesses. Some of the successes and failures were chronicled by a writer friend of mine, Robert Whiting, in a book titled: "Tokyo Underworld." This book should really have been entitled: "Doing Business in Japan." It's a great book on how business was really done in Japan after the war.

The Japanese are great at learning and they used our expertise. Few Americans worked for Japanese companies back then. Most Americans had their own businesses, but they worked with the Japanese when necessary. The Japanese would be interested in some particular American product, and they would approach an American and say: "Can you help us do that here?" So really, while there was a lot of wheeling and dealing, we were helping them.

American companies employed the Japanese, but the Japanese seldom hired American or any other foreigners back then. They had a long tradition as an insular society, and though that was beginning to change, it would take some pioneers to do it, both among the Americans, and the Japanese. Eventually I would become one of those pioneers, working for, and getting along well with Japanese employers. But that was in the future. At first I was there as an American working for Americans.

In the 1970s you could see the Japanese working hard. They could now see things getting better. This was, after all, the Japan that had only recently emerged from the ashes of B-29 raids and two atom bombs. Any adult could recall a time when Japan was utterly broke and beaten. But now they were starting to see the first signs of "The Bubble." They worked like crazy beavers.

They had a complicated system in business. There were the big companies, the small companies, and a whole labyrinth of relationships, but the bottom line was: you worked your ass off. You could see the lights burning in the new office buildings at eight, nine, and even midnight or later. But their systems were so complicated that a job that would take us eight hours would take them sixteen. Also, they had unwritten rules like: if the section chief stays you stay. So a lot of people sat in those lit-up offices doing nothing, just waiting for the boss to go home.

I thought it best for me to work into their culture gradually. As an American I wasn't cut out for all the Japanese bullshit. But I was as amazed then as I am today. My exotic taste for a different life was certainly put to the test in Japan. There is an old saying: "Be careful for what you ask for as you might just get it."

I got it all right. Japan was a whole different universe to me. Though I'd seen many other countries and their ways, I was now thrust into the center of one new Disneyland. I knew I had to adapt myself to the culture if I were to prosper. Furthermore I had a three-year contract with Automatic Electric. It was a good thing I didn't mind being stuck here. On the contrary, I couldn't get enough of this place. In Tokyo two things immediately impressed me: how expensive things were and how many beautiful women there were.

The beauty of the women offset the price of living and I found myself ready for the long haul!

Disneyland, here I come again!

5

Marriage, Family, and a New Job

If you don't want to work, you have to work to earn enough money so that you won't have to work.

—Ogden Nash

In 1970 my contract with Automated Electric was up. At that point President Nixon had pulled the plug on a lot of defense projects and people were ready to pull the plug on him. My boss said I had three choices: I could go to Chicago and work for the company on their assembly line (I said: "Right…"), or I could go up to the Arctic Circle and work on a project detecting incoming missiles, looking at radar screens for six months at a clip ("Uh huh…"), or get on a boat for six months at a time between Hawaii and Australia tracking the Apollo Shots. None of these appealed to me. I was enjoying Japanese life, and I was starting to see a future there. Then that future took a flesh-and-blood form.

I was introduced to my first wife, Taeko, in the Hilton hotel in Akasaka. I was in my thirties, and she was a couple of years younger than me. She came from a good family. They'd owned rubber factories that had been destroyed during the war. When that happened her people moved out to the country, and when they came back to the city after the war, they were broke. Everything was decimated, and all their former holdings were worthless. It was the same with many Japanese families. Lost wars do that.

If there was any money left, my wife couldn't get any of it, so she worked as a part-time model, and at night she was a hostess in one of the clubs. Her modeling career was mostly uptown stuff, and her hostess work was for businesses. She was a high-end woman. She invited me to her club, and I went. I was very taken with her. Later she said she would meet me at a hotel. Of course, once we got there one thing led to another. I was caught in that web women weave. I felt ready.

It didn't happen all at once. She wasn't as desperate to marry as some women might be. She had her modeling and her real business in the hostess clubs. She worked nights. I began to frequent her club. She was a beautiful woman, and could have had several men, but in the end I was the one she caught.

We got married at the American Embassy, which meant officially we'd married on American ground. This gave us certain advantages in both countries. We brought a witness, and in a first floor office the counselor married us. It was a simple ceremony. After that we went to the Japanese ward office to register as a married couple. That way our marriage would be official in Japan as well. She had to fill out the paperwork. In this she put her married name and my name on the Koseki Tohon (which is a document that certifies where you are, who you are, and what your legal status is. Every Japanese citizen has one.)

Her younger brother was at the wedding, and I had a friend there, a man I worked with. She had no other family there, and neither did I. Her mother had recently died. Her father had been dead for some time. The rest of her family had gone their separate ways. Over the years of our marriage we seldom saw them, except for one sister.

Taeko came from a traditional background, yet she was part of an emerging population in a nation of unmatched material wealth. She was interested in having her part of this wealth and accordingly, as the foreign male husband I was obliged to supply the material comforts. This was simply how it was. I was still young, and too immature to understand this, much less to cope with it. It wasn't the kind of marriage I had seen back at home. We had very different ways of doing things. My wife and I often disagreed. I came to see that on many matters she was right and I often was right too. It is the difference of the cultures, the clashing of East against West. But it was many years before I was able to be so philosophical about it. At the time I would get frustrated. Then I would go to work and she would do things her way.

I understood that in getting married and having a child on the way I had better settle down. This was doubly hard because now I would be settling into both a culture and a situation that were entirely new to me. Suddenly I had to learn many things Japanese, things I hadn't really paid much attention to before. At the same time I was trying to find a job. I was ready to take almost anything.

Since leaving Automated Electric I'd done several things. Getting married was just one of them. I had tried my hand at selling cars, getting a job as a salesman with a dealer on the base where we were living. We were on Tachikawa base, which was a military installation that had gone through some cosmetic conversion. The Army had leased it to an airplane company called Tachikawa Aircraft Corp. We were living there in a house that had one back entrance onto the base, and a front entrance off the base to the street. My wife's friends were mainly out the entrance that led to the street outside the base. She was very Japanese with little international experience except for marrying me. She learned enough English to get along, but no more. Most of the people who lived around there were foreigners. Some were government workers; others sold cars, while some were insurance people who were selling to other people on the base. We were a whole mix of different people doing different things.

My son Justin was born the year after we married. We raised him both ways. He went to Japanese schools, and Taeko acted as a Japanese mother, but I taught him too, and I tended toward a more American approach. I got my two cents in, but all in all he was raised more as a Japanese boy. I had no problem with this. After all, here he was, born in this country, and most of the people he knew were Japanese from when he was small. Yet Justin's life with me was not a normal one, not even for the son of a mixed marriage in Japan. I was very much a maverick, and knew what it was to be a foreigner. I remained an American, but figured out ways to win the trust of the Japanese. I was my own man, and not simply a western version of a Japanese "salaryman". (A "salaryman" is really just a white-collar worker—one more Japanese fracture of an American concept.)

I did things my own way in Japan, partially because I knew it would pay off eventually, but more because it was the only sensible way for me to do things. This was something the Japanese came to respect, and in return they knew I respected their ways. Marriage and my own selling abilities helped me find a niche in Japanese society. When a client came from the West I could do things the normal American in Japan could not. I could show him both worlds.

But that was just beginning in the early 1970s. All I knew then was that I had to find a way to support my family. It was during this time that I stopped selling cars, and went down to Tokyo. I finally discovered that city, and soon it would discover me.

6

Understanding a New Land

A successful man is one who makes more money than his wife can spend. A successful woman is one who can find such a man.

—Lana Turner

At this point in my life, as with men who father children throughout the world, I focused on the essentials: making money.

I heard there were jobs teaching English, and people told me I was qualified to do it. This surprised the shit out of me. I had never thought about teaching English as a second language. I'd never thought of myself as any kind of teacher. A street kid from Brooklyn seldom does. But we Brooklyn boys are always ready to try something new, especially if there's a buck involved.

In Japan if you could speak English, you could teach it. If you were a German, but spoke passable English, your students would come out of your class speaking like a bunch of Bavarian brew masters. If you were French they might sound like a Japanese Maurice Chevalier. I guess my students wound up speaking Brooklyn-ese, which no doubt served them well if they ever got off the subway in Flatbush. These Japanese students weren't worried about strange sounding accents; they were learning how to talk dollars and cents. They needed English the same way a salesman needs his order book.

I applied for a job in a school in central Tokyo over the phone. The demand was such that they hired me as a temp teacher without even laying eyes on me. I may have been only a temp, but I quickly learned that this was a big opportunity. There was even some money in it. In my first class I taught forty young businessmen, all of whom were working for a start-up computer company. In the late 1960s Japan stood at the cutting edge of computer technology, and they were about to show the world what they had. These forty young men were a part of an army that was about the change the face of international markets.

As an American it was a curious phenomenon to witness. It was my country that they were challenging, but this was not Pearl Harbor. The conflict was in the business world and this battle's resolution would lead to more riches for everyone. This time Japan recognized that the battle lines were bottom lines.

In English class I would stand behind a podium, holding a textbook. My students would watch me and I would watch them. As I taught them how to say "yes" and "no," I kept asking myself: "What the hell am I doing here?" I learned to shrug it off, and taught them to say: "maybe." It worked. They learned.

These Japanese learned English quicker than I learned their language. They were on a mission. Though I was trying to settle down and fit in, I couldn't help but just enjoy myself. I learned enough to get by. If you're going to live in another country, and deal with its people you should always learn enough of the language to do business, both for convenience, and to give the people you're speaking to the respect they deserve. To this day, I don't speak too much Japanese, and I regret that. In my day most Americans did not take learning Japanese seriously. Today with a global economy, and more complex business practices many learn Japanese before they even get here. They feel they need it to compete. But though they get here knowing the language, they really have no knowledge of the culture. This is the New World, my friend.

While I learned the necessities of language by osmosis, I was certainly learning the culture in everything I did. I was learning it in the school, and I was learning it in my marriage. I had married a hostess from a club. I had married a country girl who had come to the city. I had married a woman whose family had once had money and now it was gone. It was all pretty complex. And I wasn't too easy to figure out either. Mavericks never are.

Foreign readers might wonder exactly what a hostess is. Many people get hostesses mixed up with geishas. There is a parallel between the two, but only in that they are two roles for single women in the same society. Also, both are defined by their relationship to men. But from there on the similarities shrink.

There are miles of difference between a geisha and a hostess. The Geisha is brought up in a geisha house by a mama, who is a geisha herself. The mama trains the girl until she is ready to go out and entertain in any geisha house. The geisha wears a kimono. She can dance, sing, play games. Hand games and word games are among the favorites.

An ordinary hostess wears beautiful clothes, but her job is just to sit and entertain the men who come in. The customers aren't supposed to fondle them. That's part of the system. A geisha is likely to remain a geisha for life. Even if she marries a man, she carries the art of the geisha into her home. It governs the way she socializes, and when she does it well this is admired by all. That's her system. When I first got here you might still see a geisha in her carriage, riding through Tokyo. Some were quite old, but there was an artistic beauty about them.

These are truly a special type of women. One western misconception is that they are simply prostitutes. The American or European will tend to look at any woman whose job begins with the idea of pleasing a male audience with her femininity, and assume she is some kind of whore. While some geishas may have taken their role into something like high-class prostitution, most of them don't. It's all in the system: Once again, remember the training the geisha has received in the geisha house from her mama. The mama has put time, effort and money into making a girl into a perfect geisha. It is not an easy process, and it takes money for upkeep, and a great deal of time and effort. So if some rich man does come along, and wants this girl as a wife, or as a mistress, then he must pay the mama for this huge investment. If this is prostitution, so be it, but it has also been a part of a social system that has worked for many centuries. It's a system like any other social system, and you really must respect that.

Most of the geishas come from farm families. In earlier days the farmers often sold their daughters because they couldn't afford them anymore. And, of course, many girls decided this was what they wanted to do. This may sound cruel to the modern foreigner, but it wasn't long ago that daughters were regarded the same way in the west, and others were bought and sold far more brutally only a little more than a century ago. In Japan these girls were being given a chance for a far more interesting and comfortable life. If you judge it by freedom, the geisha may have had more than the farm woman. Now such practices as selling daughters have changed in Japan, but the art of the geisha—which is a true art like any other—is being lost.

So how does this relate to hostesses? As I've said, they are both roles where women entertain men with femininity, but there the similarities end. The Japanese people see the Geisha as an artist creating a carefully thought-out impression, like a painter using palate and canvass. They look at a hostess as being a job. Hostesses aren't looked down on. They're part of the Mizu Shobai world. Mizu Shobai means "water business" which means the Club Business. The Club business here in Japan is one of the biggest grossing businesses in the country. For many decades hostess clubs have been a mainstay of urban economies here. The world of hostess clubs is somewhat diminished now because the young women have become more independent. But the world of hostesses is still big, and the new glamour is in the foreign hostesses. Girls from Britain, America, New Zealand or Australia come here, make some money, and they don't really have to do much for it. Most of them are only here for three to six months, the length of a working visa (or for some, a tourist visa).

But traditionally the hostess served up a particularly Japanese brand of femininity. They were there to serve the men, and give them a little fun. It wasn't a well-learned discipline, as it was in a geisha house. It was simply the traditional Japanese woman in a sexy, club atmosphere.

Could you take her to a hotel? Often you could, and I'll go into that in more detail in the next chapter. For like everything else in Japan, that takes place within a carefully defined system.

And do Japanese wives complain when their husbands go to these places? Either the geisha house, or the hostess club? My wife, Taeko never did, nor did most of the wives of her generation. Of course she never asked and I never said, but it was expected that the Japanese businessman would entertain guests at these clubs. She had been a hostess. Both of us knew how it worked, and there was no shame or stigma in it. Our problems weren't about other women. Traditional Japanese wives understand that it's part of the system, so they don't care. They never mention it. My problems with Taeko were cultural and personal. Maybe neither of us was ready for marriage, and if we had been ready, we wouldn't have married each other. But you never know these things when you need to.

Western guys come over here and see these beautiful Japanese girls, and watch them serving men, and they're magnetically attracted to that inborn sense of what a Japanese woman is. Any man wants that kind of treatment. Hell, I certainly did. But when you marry them that changes a little bit. Then you have certain obligations, and you had better fulfill them. At that point a hard-edged materialism becomes the rule in many marriages. It certainly did in mine.

The biggest single thing in a traditional Japanese woman's life is security. So as long as a man takes care of that, he can go out and do whatever he likes. Just come home with the bacon. That is changing, and in many ways that's good. Some women go back to work, even after they have kids. Many women now will quietly complain about the old way of life, whether it be hostess clubs or Japanese men not wearing wedding bands. They wait longer than in other countries. But that wasn't true of us. After all that was thirty years ago. Back then the world was different. Back then I took some crazy jobs to help keep my family secure. Working for a Japanese gun dealer named the "Merchant of Death" was one of those jobs.

I'll talk about that next.

7

Working in the Hostess Clubs

Everyone plays golf now, which is a lot like going to a strip club. You get all charged up, pay big money to hang out on a beautiful course, and start drinking early. Eighteen holes later you're plastered and frustrated and most of your balls are missing.

—Tim Allen

Soon after my wife got pregnant I took up a job working at the Foreign Language Institute language school which was right in the middle of the entertainment district of Ginza Tokyo. Ginza is filled with after-work hostess clubs and high-end shops. Back in the '70s Tokyo was expensive but not like today. Now Tokyo is the most expensive city in the world. Tokyo Ginza is so expensive that just 3.3 square meters of property goes for about a million dollars.

My boss in Ginza was a retired sergeant in the American Air Force. We had both been in the American military and we were both from New York. We immediately became fast friends. I enjoyed my work at the school, and he liked having me. After three months, he put me on a regular salary. I wasn't satisfied with just teaching. I decided to start selling English classes to Japanese companies. This was the beginning of a tendency that has been with me ever since: Though I sometimes rock the boat a little, I get on well with my Japanese colleagues. I understand them. It was also the first inkling of my career in selling.

My boss was an American who had stayed in Japan after retiring. I was doing almost the same thing. He'd married a Japanese stewardess who had worked for Air France and had started the school with her.

40

He was affectionately known as "The Merchant of Death" by the police because he imported old guns. One of his clients was Mr.Shimizu, who owned one of the high-end clubs called Appolian, just a few blocks up from the school.

One day my boss called me in. There he had a set of antique French dueling pistols that he'd bought. He asked me if I would take these guns, and put them up on the wall at Shimizu's club. These pistols were obviously for display, and what better place for them but the walls of a hostess club.

I went there to deliver the pistols, and that was when I met Shimizu. He owned the place. Shimizu was pro-American in both attitude and outlook. He liked talking with an American like me. My errand with the dueling pistols became the first of many visits. Often I would go there in the late afternoon, before he opened the club. We would sit in the place while they were getting ready to open the door and Shimizu and I would talk about anything that came up. We got to be pretty good friends. All this was going on while I was still selling, and teaching English to all the young, ambitious Japanese guys. Some of those guys were Shimizu's customers, or if they weren't, their bosses were. This was, after all, a high-end club.

One day Shimizu asked me if I wanted a part time job. He said: "How would you like to be a bartender?" I thought about that for a moment, and said: "Sure." Why shouldn't I? He seemed like a decent guy, and we got along. I had never bartended before, but it didn't look as if it was too hard. I never had any doubts that I could do the work.

Shimizu was only open from 7 to 11 in the evening. Those were the hours when men from Japanese companies were out looking for female companionship. For me the hours were perfect. I could work for "The Merchant of Death," teaching English and carrying his antique guns in the afternoon, then bartend among a lot of beautiful women at night. For awhile I worked both jobs. Working at the language school, and moonlighting as a bartender didn't bother me at all. Hell, it was fun.

But if I was moving in any direction, it was toward the entertainment business.

My job at Club Appolian was straightforward. I made hostess drinks, mostly tea served up in whiskey glasses. This was what they drank at thirty bucks a pop. The customers had a pretty good idea of what was going on, and if they didn't they picked it up real fast. They knew they were paying more for the hostess's attentions than for the contents of her glass. The only time we deviated from this was when the customer insisted to the girl: "I want you to have a real drink with me," which forced the issue. Then I'd pour something with a shot of alcohol in it, and she would drink it. I didn't make it strong. There may have been some customers who didn't understand this system, but not many. The guys who came in there drank heavily. I sold a lot of drinks. There I could make 10,000 yen in four hours (about $140 in those days). At that time it was a lot of money.

Eventually I quit teaching at the school, but I knew that job had helped me. To a Brooklyn boy teaching was an ego-booster. Also, it was the first time I'd really sold a service to anyone. I found I wasn't a bad salesman. The school helped me slowly break into real Japanese culture. The club provided me with a further education of Japanese culture.

Shimizu employed about thirty Japanese women as hostesses. He also had a few foreign hostesses, though these were rare at that time. In the early 1970s Japan was still very much a country for its own people. We foreigners were few, and there were many occupations, which were reserved only for the Japanese. Today there are a lot more foreign women working in the clubs (American, Philippine, Russian, British, etc.)

In those days each of these Japanese hostesses made about twenty-to-thirty thousand yen per evening, the equivalent of about $450 today. A girl did this in about five hours. The club's clientele included the middle and upper management of most of Tokyo's leading trading companies. These were the men who ran companies like Mitsubishi,

Sumitomo, and Mitsui. They had plenty of money. They sat at my bar and spent it. Money was never exchanged with the girls, and there were many transactions where I didn't collect cash. Customers just signed for it. At the end of the month the club would bill the man's company. The amount of each bill reflected the man's standing in the company. The higher your rank, the more you spent (and the more we charged for the same service). It was a unique system to say the least. They called it the Expense Account System. I called it: Tap the Rich. It's a system that has lost ground recently. Since the Bubble popped many companies have become much more careful with their entertainment budgets. Easy entertainment money is harder to get.

That was how it worked with our regular clientele. With those whom we seldom saw, and with foreigners, most clubs operated on a case-by-case basis. New patrons and most foreigners were usually served on the pay-as-you-go method. Those were almost the only times I saw cash.

If a man kept going back to the same club and repeatedly requested the same girl, the owner would tell her that, if he wanted, she would be required to sleep with him. If that happened then the customer would pay the girl about fifty thousand yen, plus hotel room, and taxi. That would add another fifty thousand yen to the tab (take out charge), making the cost of the night about a thousand dollars in today's money. This was standard house policy in the better hostess clubs

The hostesses had a certain level of potential mobility within the establishments. They could work their way up and out of the clubs. For example, an older executive might buy an apartment for a hostess. For a hostess this was often her highest aspiration and dream. Then she would become his mistress and he could visit her during the day. This usually meant that she no longer worked at the club. Some Japanese executives still pride themselves by picking up side apartments for their girlfriends. Though this is done in the US and other countries, it's more in tune with Japanese culture.

My role was to serve the drinks for the hostesses inside, and speak English to the clientele at the bar. Before entering the lounge, these Japanese businessmen would practice their English on me. This new kind of "English teaching" gave me a dual function, which my customers saw as an extra benefit in coming to the club. Many of them thought of me more as an English teacher than a bartender. Some knew that I had recently been a teacher of my native language, and would stay at the bar speaking English with me. It happened enough that some of the hostesses complained about it. I was cutting into their time and money. This was after all, a Hostess club, not a language school. The girls made me promise to send these guys back to the lounge area where they would drink more and spend more money. The more they spent, the larger the hostesses' tips. Their clients even tipped me at times. The owner didn't mind at all. He was very pro-American.

This was an upscale establishment with an average of seventy-five to a hundred clients per night spending over a thousand dollars apiece for a three-hour stay. If you do the math you can see that the club was grossing the equivalent of over twenty million dollars per year. And that was just one club. It was an example of the staggering scope of the entertainment industry in Tokyo. This holds true to this day. It is an industry that has done a lot for me, and I have always tried to do the same for it in return.

This entertainment industry has spread throughout Tokyo and there are many different pockets, like the Ginza nightclub district. Each has its own personality. The Roppongi of today has a foreign flavor, and is a favorite of tourists. This entertainment machine spills out into the rural areas, and through the small towns. They too have their hostess clubs and bars where a young man can get a drink, and spend long hours with a pretty young girl. There are few foreign girls in the countryside. The money's not there.

This is the system and it works. It keeps the crazies off the street. When a young guy can go in, and have a girl rub his knees, and make him feel good, it keeps him from going out in the street and making real trouble. In other countries some idiot guys at that age go out, grab a woman, and some even commit rape. That doesn't normally happen here. Tokyo is one of the safest cities, and Japan is one of the safest countries in the world. I think that's because the young men here have an outlet.

During all those early years of living it up and having fun, I got drunk, missed my train, and went and slept in the park more than once. No one ever came near me. I was as safe as I would have been in my own home. How many countries can make that claim? That's changed a little, as western things come in. But basically it's still a very safe place.

In the early 1970s it was safe, and yet it was exciting too. It was a country just waking up to its own possibilities. And I was there waking up with it.

8

In the Years Before the Bubble

Do you think God knew what he was doing when he created Woman? Or was it just another one of his tiny mistakes like earthquakes, tidal waves, floods?

—**Jack Nicholson** in *The Witches of Eastwick*

Tokyo has changed drastically since I first came here. Physically it's a different place. One of the main parts of Tokyo, a place called Shinjuku was nothing at all back then. In those days the KDD Building and the Keio Plaza Hotel were the biggest buildings there. Everything else was small. In the back of the Keio Hotel was an old wastewater plant that they had filled in. I went there to see the Barnum & Bailey Circus. They brought that over here around 1970. In 34 years that area has grown incredibly. Now there's a skyline of skyscrapers.

When the Bubble started the building started. The most famous developer, Mori has built sixty-plus buildings now. These are all commercial buildings up to 18 stories. He also built Ark Hills, a huge development of upscale living. In the old days it was nothing but small mom & pop shops.

He recently built a place called Roppongi Hills. It opened up in April, 2003. This was one of the most expensive development projects in the world. At the top of this magnificent 54-story building is the "Mori Art Museum". There you can experience the art and culture of Tokyo at the same time. There is a slick orange bar near the gallery where you can relax and see surrounding Tokyo. The view is like none in the world. In another space-age part of the building there is the Virgin Cinemas, with 12 screens. Part of this complex looks like something from Star Wars. There is a Premier Screen, which is as big as any in the world with luxury seating. There are restaurants, shops, houses, apartments, hotels...the difference is unbelievable, and in some cases so is the price. The Hyatt Hotel has a presidential suite that goes for $3,800 a night. The condos rent for as high as $32,000 a month.

If you don't stop by the Roppongi Hills you haven't really seen the new Japan.

Many of the older buildings are from The Bubble. Different people define this era differently. Some say it began before 1980. Some say it lasted into the mid-1990s. But all can agree that from about 1983 to the early 1990s there was a boom like Japan had never seen. Money was everywhere. If you had a project that seemed remotely possible, you could find backing. That was The Bubble.

An example of how things were different during The Bubble was how the taxies operated. There were so many jobs that no one really needed to be a cab driver. There were lots of jobs. It got so difficult to get a cab late at night that if you could not flash a 5,000 yen note no one would pick you up (5,000 yen was about 75 bucks back then). Even if the ride would normally cost 1,000 yen you could not get a ride unless you were spending 5,000 yen. The cabs were making a killing. Now there are so many cabs in the streets you get two or three trying to compete to stop and pick you up. In the ten years since, many of these new drivers have been laid off.

But even before those amazing Bubble years Japan wasn't standing still. For almost four decades this country had been rebuilding from the War, then rebuilding again. There had been ups and downs, but the Japan I came to in 1968 was getting richer. A few years later, as I entered the business world of Tokyo the country was growing richer still.

The Tokyo of the early 1970s was on a smaller scale, yet all the signs were there. The Japanese people had already built a thriving economy manufacturing products for the United States and Europe. Little Datsun trucks and Hondas were already being shipped across the Pacific, challenging the Big Three car companies of my home country. It was about to become a flood. Those cars and trucks were small, but they also burned less gas, and that was about to become an issue worldwide. The Japanese have always had to import every drop of oil, so they know how to conserve instinctively. Americans were still driving Cutlasses, Fairlanes, and El Dorados. When the crunch came, there would be all those fuel-efficient Japanese cars—inexpensive to buy, and to run. As Americans bought these up a whole new wave of dollars came across the ocean to Japan.

Compared to where they'd been in the years after the War, the Japanese were already rich. But they weren't going to stop there. The new American and European dollars were the seed money. It wasn't there yet, but it was coming.

It was during this time, that I left the hostess clubs, and started selling advertising. There were more possibilities, and more chances for advancement. Maybe there was more room for a maverick as well…

I was a young married man living in the suburbs of Tokyo. At first I bartended in the hostess club, which had me in Tokyo, but then I sold cars on the military bases for awhile. That kept me out near where we were living. My wife, Taeko got pregnant, and I knew I would have even more responsibilities soon. This was Japan. There was no question of wives working. I was the breadwinner, and I accepted this as part of the system. But I had to find new ways to win the bread. Selling cars wasn't the answer.

At that point I realized there were problems with my learning curve. There were many things I didn't know how to do, or couldn't do, because I was living so far out in the suburbs. But then I realized I could take things I knew—my street smarts—and use them in Tokyo. I felt very much at home down in the city. Why wouldn't a boy who'd grown up in New York?

While I was still bartending I met a man at an embassy party. It was an encounter that would change the course of my employment. His name was Miyata. Miyata owned a publishing company and he was looking for a foreigner to be a salesman for his publications. In the 1970s it was unusual for a Japanese company to hire a foreigner, but this fellow was different. He had plans to add an international profile to his business. I didn't want to be an English-teaching, bartending, car dealer forever, and this guy's business plan appealed to me, so I went to work for him.

The company Miyata owned was the Business Word Corporation. Working there was really the start of my commercial life in Japan. When I started selling advertising I was selling for three publications. The first was the *Escort Tokyo Guide Map*, written in English. It was given away free to hotels, restaurants, and clubs that catered to foreigners. These maps were subsidized by advertising.

The second publication was a tabloid called the *Escort Shimbun,* a guide to entertainment that was all in Japanese ("Shimbun" means "newspaper" in Japanese). This "shimbun" also went to hotels and restaurants, but was aimed at those serving tourists from Japan. Locals might pick this up as well. After all, Tokyo was a huge town, and no one could know it completely. *Escort* was a giveaway too.

Then there was a quarterly magazine called *Happy Wedding Magazine*. This was the only magazine that wasn't free of charge. We got ads from people in wedding-related businesses. The caterers at a wedding ball would run pictures of the wedding, but these would be ads, and they'd pay the same way you do for any ad. The same would go for entertainers, the photographers, and any other service people providing for the big day's festivities.

A salesman's job was to go out and get the ads. This wasn't as simple as it sounds. Selling ads was hard work. In fact it may have been the most difficult work I'd ever done. You had to keep up your sales totals or you'd be out. I made plenty of calls where I went in with high hopes, and left empty-handed. Miyata wasn't the sympathetic type either. He wanted sales. He was tough as nails, but he taught me how to sell in the street. He brought out the street smart Brooklyn boy, and he didn't mind that I was a maverick. He expected me to sell to clubs, restaurants, companies, and anywhere else I could.

It took me three months to make my first sale. He almost fired me on many occasions, but in the end he always stuck by me. He was my *sensei*.

If Miyata hadn't toughened me up I might never have become a success. He always complained about my presentation, but I learned through his criticism. Within two years, I was making over 800,000 yen (about $12,000) a month, and had a sales team of my own. Every one knew me. They welcomed me in every club and disco. I was the only foreigner doing this kind of business in Tokyo. I was becoming a top dog in the Roppongi business district.

But that took time.

When I started out most of the ads I generated were for the English guide map, but soon I was selling for the *Escort* tabloid too. I had sales kits for both. I'd go to the entertainment areas and buildings. In Tokyo we have buildings that are purely entertainment from the top floor on down. I would go in the evenings, start on the top floor of an entertainment building, and work my way down. I'd begin my rounds at seven, before they opened. I'd work until about eleven, then catch an hour's train ride home. At that point I was still a Tokyo suburbanite. Like most people who work in town, I didn't live there.

I was with the publishing house for six years

In those years I paid a lot of attention to my son. I took him to the park, and to baseball games, then he got involved in Little League. But I got to the point where I wasn't particularly interested in my wife. She became too materialistic. I wasn't ready for that. It wasn't really her fault, or my fault. It was just a lot of things that led to this cultural misunderstanding. Maybe some of it was being a maverick, but that was in my Brooklyn blood.

I liked drinking, I liked smoking, and I liked other women. I had a man's appetites. I wanted to do the things I'd been accustomed to doing all my adult life. As a result all of a sudden I didn't really want to live with my wife anymore. More and more I didn't return home at night. I spent most of my time in Tokyo, going out with my friends, and spending time with all kinds of different women, then catching the last train home.

Sometimes I missed that last train. I might remain in Tokyo, and stay up till all hours with friends, including lady friends. There were also those nights when I slept undisturbed in the park. This sometimes seemed better than going home.

My wife didn't give me any problems about this, and I guess that surprised me a little. Maybe it bothered me too. I had a westerner's expectations about marriage. I assumed Taeko would be jealous of the other women, and that would make her angry at my staying away. But the older generation Japanese women don't do that. They simply run the house. What they ask for is ample resources to keep the home in order. As long as those are provided, they don't mind a husband wandering. They assume he will. (This is not as true today for some young Japanese women who will cut their husband's balls off if they catch them doing what I did. Young Japanese men, watch your nuts!)

I would get upset with my wife because of the way she dealt with things. It was the Japanese system, but I didn't understand that yet. I adjusted to her lack of jealousy, but there were a thousand other details to this system. One thing was their custom concerning presents. I didn't get that at all.

It starts like this: in your apartment complex, or your neighborhood, your neighbor might give you two apples. Then you have to give him three oranges, to which he might respond with four pears. This gamesmanship is the wife's responsibility, and a good wife will know how to work the gifts so you are always getting more than you're giving. It is a skill that is part social niceties, and part accounting, but it is important to be ahead. If you're not careful you end up in a vicious cycle of gift-giving hell. The fun dies when it becomes a duty. The Japanese love duty, honor and saving face. This can drive a maverick nuts.

The gift system is a holdover from country life that has carried over into the city. But I didn't understand it at all. Now I do understand the system. It's alright with me, and I agree with it. But at that time it was just one more thing irritating our marriage.

But I had my work and my life in Tokyo. I've been lucky in that I've always enjoyed doing business, any kind of business. I liked selling the entertainment ads. It was something I was good at. Because of that my business led me to spend a great deal of time on the Roppongi, Tokyo's fabled entertainment district. I was there often, and I became well-known in that community.

My first real experience in the important clubs came in a place called the Copacabana in Akasaka, a very snazzy place. All the American entertainers loved that club: Frank Sinatra, Dean Martin, Sammy Davis, and all the Rat Pack. When they were in Japan they could be counted on to show up at The Copacabana. This place was truly high-end, the kind of club where the top mob guys might rub shoulders with members of the Cabinet.

The Copacabana was run by a woman named Mama Cherry. She was like a grandmother. She was famous beyond Tokyo. When I first met her she was nearing sixty, and had been in the club business for most of her life. She'd worked the hostess clubs, and had been a hostess herself, so she knew every trick of the trade. Finally she'd opened up this place, and was earning a great reputation almost overnight. From there on it was golden. She built several buildings including the Noa Building. There was one red brick building she built which was round, and very tall, with small windows, just a huge red tower thrusting up into the air. Of course, it invited the usual jokes. People said Mama Cherry's building seemed strangely familiar. Didn't it look just like the thing that had built it? It was a joke that wasn't far from the truth.

There in her club Mama Cherry was a monarch. She hired the girls, told them what to do, arranged for outside liaisons, got people hotel rooms, and did all the things a queen monarch does for her subjects. She attended to every detail.

Mama Cherry was a smart businesswoman. Somewhere along the line she'd learned to keep a certain distance from her clientele. When you came in she'd be sitting at a table in the corner. She sat in that corner, and remained somewhat remote and foreign—once again, like a monarch. But she had her guys and girls working for her. They all knew exactly what they were supposed to do, and they did it. She made sure it was obvious to anyone who entered that this was no ordinary club. The waiters wore tuxedos.

The Copacabana had an upstairs and a downstairs. All the girls sat upstairs, either waiting for their customers to come in, or waiting to be assigned to someone. When someone new came in Mama would link him up with the right girl. Downstairs was a wide spread of beautifully laid out tables. When you entered there was no question that this was a special place.

When a regular customer arrived the headwaiter would bring down the desired girl and seat her with her patron. You might want to take your choice of girls. If you'd been there before this might be an option. All of the girls were beautiful, and they dressed to the nines.

All of this was at a time when the girls were Japanese. A few foreigners were already in the hostess business, but their clubs were small. The Copa had the whole nine yards, dancers, singers—all of it, and it was always presented with class.

Over time I got to know Mama Cherry quite well. I never got pushy with her. That would've been fatal with Mama Cherry. You didn't just breeze in and sit down at her table. I would sit at the upstairs bar talking with friends. She would often come through, stop, and talk with me. We talked about some of her famous customers, and she would ask how I was doing. She even offered me a job.

As an American the doors would usually have been closed to relationships like this one. Foreigners were put in a separate class. But I was working for a Japanese man in a business that was local. That was unusual. With it the door swung open, and I could become friends with someone like Mama Cherry. Mama Cherry only advertised with us once, but her contribution to my business career went well beyond that. I learned from her. Also the connection was golden. Slowly but surely I was becoming the King of Roppongi.

9

The King of Roppongi

I am the Lizard King...I can do anything.

—**Jim Morrison** (1943–1971)

There was a time when people knew of the six trees that gave Roppongi its name. I've never seen them. The kanji translation of Roppongi is literally "Six Trees" (If you really want to be specific and break down the 3 kanji, one word is "6", the other is "book" and the last is "tree". I am not sure where the book comes from—but hell, sometimes the Japanese can't even explain their own kanji.)

Roppongi isn't a huge area but it does have an interesting history. A lot of young kids who party in that town's entertainment district don't know that a lot of people died there because we Americans blanketed it with Napalm in World War II. This tragedy was worse than that of the Great Hanshin Earthquake. The bombs converted the section into a Dresden-like inferno. More people died in the fire bombing of Tokyo than in the American atomic bombings of both Hiroshima and Nagasaki. War is hell, and don't let anyone tell you any different.

Roppongi is only about nine blocks long, and about three or four blocks deep. But it is an area all its own. It's lit up at night like any of the major entertainment areas of the world. Paris, Atlantic City, and Las Vegas have nothing on the Roppongi. It's the center of entertainment, and since entertainment is one of the biggest taxpaying industries in Japan, the Roppongi is also one of the biggest taxpayers. The Japanese government feeds off entertainment.

I hung out in Roppongi from my earliest days in Tokyo, but it was while I was working for Miyata that people first referred to me as the "King of Roppongi". My business took me into all the clubs and bars, and I got to know all the people there. I couldn't walk down the street without people calling out: "Oh, Roa-san."

Roppongi has gone through many facelifts since I got here. In the '70s it was an elegant place with stylish clubs. Flashy discos were just opening. In the '80s that changed. The clubs became more open. The Japanese girls and hostesses seemed younger in that decade, more college age. And now, with The Bubble burst, the young men of Africa have discovered Roppongi. They often work as shills outside the clubs, handing out pamphlets promoting the places. The streets of Roppongi are now filled with Nigerian guys, and there are foreign hostess clubs where the girls are exclusively from other countries. All of it has changed, which is a normal state of affairs. I expect in the future it will again.

In the days when I was "King of Roppongi" everyone knew me because of my business. At first the publications made me visible. People wanted to get into them, and for that they came to me. As I went into business for myself many of the discos wanted to start special programs of their own promoting themselves, and I helped in this. I had a finger in everything, and my ear was to the ground. I had information, and information is power. It made them call me: "King." It was a name given to me. When I would go into a disco there was always a table, or a seat at the bar reserved for Rick-san. I would walk down the street, and in any given block twenty or thirty people would call out: "Rick-san". When friends from outside the district would walk there with me they would say: "Rick, how do you know so many people?" Well, I was the King.

All of us were helping each other out. Being King I certainly got my share of this. In plenty of places the drinks would come, or the food would arrive, and they'd say: "It's on the house, Rick-san. We'll take care of it, Rick-san." I did my part. I was always bringing business their way, sending plenty of people with money into their clubs and restaurants, and they were thankful.

At the Playboy Club they had foreign singers who would come to play. They would be here on three-month visas. So every three months the club would have a new singer, and every three months I'd have a new girl friend. I was famous in the Playboy Club. They knew my influence in the embassies, so they would often give me carte blanche with a few free memberships which I could bestow upon those I deemed deserving. That way I could be their ambassador to the Ambassadors. It was important to them to be able to have a place to bring their clients. After all, socializing in a convivial atmosphere is an important part of the game of international relations. This way the Playboy Club was always a stop for such people. It was a big club, taking up one big floor in the Roi Building. In Japanese "Roi" is pronounced the same as "Roa". Because of this many people thought I owned the place.

Most of the bunnies were from Tokyo, or the surrounding areas. A lot of them were girls in school. Were the bunnies like hostesses? Certainly. The same unwritten rules applied, though maybe in a more western way. That doesn't mean the bunnies were prostitutes. Out-and-out prostitution was rare back then in Tokyo, at any level. The system itself allowed enough freedom that there wasn't as much need for simple pay-for-sex. That is one of the things that, sadly, have changed here. Nowadays prostitution is very big. There are girls, particularly foreign girls, hustling on the streets of Tokyo.

In my own life at this time I was married, but my wife wasn't a part of my day-to-day life. We both accepted our separation, and I sent money home for her and my son. That was one responsibility I always took seriously, and always fulfilled. Taeko was an excellent mother, and knew how to raise a boy in the Japanese way. Though I may have introduced a good deal of Western influence into his life, I wanted Justin to grow up basically as a Japanese boy. After all, it was the country where he was born.

My own life centered as much around nights as it did days. It was the nature of my business. I sold whatever had to be sold during the day and into the evening. At night I played. I drank and smoked with the boys, and chased the women. I had girlfriends and more girlfriends. I had women running in and out of my apartment on a schedule. There was nothing odd in this. It was expected. It was a part of the system, and it was definitely a part that I could live with.

While I learned the social system I also got an education in the business system. My first boss in business, Miyata-san, came from the old school of selling, and he taught me how to be tenacious and persistent, but the most important thing he taught me was how to sell to the Japanese. He taught me to think like they do. He showed me how to make a presentation to a Japanese client that made the client comfortable. That way, though there was no question that I was a foreigner, I had a less foreign flavor.

I didn't always use this method. No method is right for every occasion, Sometimes I wanted to emphasize my foreignness, maybe show that I knew things a Japanese man wouldn't. I might give an impression of ignorance which could make the buyer feel more confident, thinking he was smarter than me. But Miyata-san gave me the know-how I needed to judge things like that. He was very tough, but his training left me sure of myself, which was invaluable. With that I could get appointments over the telephone, then meet the clients personally, and close the sale. It led me in a direction that I wouldn't have taken otherwise. Because of Miyata I was able to get out in that world and meet people. It was a job that fit my personality completely. I liked selling.

I've mentioned that I met Miyata-san at an embassy party. Tokyo was one of the great capitals of the world, so there were many embassies. Embassies anywhere do much of their work by means of social events. The embassy parties I went to were an experience I'd never expected. Remember, I was a kid off the streets of Brooklyn. We had to go all the way to Manhattan just to see City Hall. The borough office was as close as there was to an embassy. But these were the representatives of all the great nations showing off for each other. It was a spectacle.

So how did I get into such a position? At first it was just the luck of knowing somebody. Then I became a part of the publishing business, and all the embassies wanted space, free, or sometimes paid for. I might talk with the Ambassador from Kuwait one night, and the Prime Minister of Zambia the next. It was a thrill at first, but in time I came to consider it as normal.

The Saudis had some of the best parties. It was a time when the oil money was really beginning to flow. They'd have receptions at the old Imperial Hotel, the one with the Frank Lloyd Wright design that had withstood both of Tokyo's major twentieth century earthquakes. Most of the embassies used that hotel for their best receptions. The attractions were the food, the drink, and all the amazing people you could meet. It got to where I had to decide which embassy to go to each night: I made my choice on the basis of who had the best food, the best drinks, or who had the best guests. It was networking for me.

The timing couldn't have been more perfect. I was learning my craft, I was also beginning to work the embassies, and just as this was happening the discos and the Playboy Club were opening their doors.

Japan is an important nation in an important part of the world, so most countries have embassies there. They would have special events, and I would often be invited. It was the time of the Cold War, and Tokyo was a place of great intrigue. I was invited to many affairs where, if you looked closely, you saw the surface of all this. I was always one to observe a situation. When you watch long enough, and keep your ears open, you begin to see the links. I knew that if the American Ambassador was huddled deep in conversation with the Saudi military attaché that meant the Saudis were close to getting the air defense systems they'd wanted. That, in turn, meant oil prices would drop. *The Times* would have the story the following month, but I could've read it off the lips of those whom I was watching.

It was fascinating. At one point I even met Arafat. This was when the Palestinians weren't recognized by any major world powers. I had a friend who was a counselor in the Jordanian embassy, a die-hard Palestinian, but a nice guy. He got me in, though I was checked and double-checked.

I was still selling advertising at this point. All the embassies here in Japan had a voracious appetite for favorable publicity: something written, or pictures taken at their receptions. Social reviews seemed to be their lifeblood. Something—anything that put them in a good light was clipped out, and set in a little folder. Once the folder was full it was sent back to their government via diplomatic pouch. Then someone in power on the other side of the world would say: "Look at what a great job our ambassador is doing. He's promoting our country to the Japanese." I guess there was some value to it, but for me it just meant an endless string of great parties, and all the free drinks I could hold.

Once I'd been selling for the advertising company for a few years I felt as if I'd learned the ropes. I was ready to go on my own. I had my own ideas about things, and it was time. So I started doing public relations work and promotion for the big discos that were so popular then. Most of them wanted to attract more foreigners to their clubs. I would print up tickets, go out among the foreigners in town, and hand out the tickets at a discount.

Through all of this, my money situation was improving. That had been true all through my years of selling advertising, and it was true now.

By the early eighties I was, for all intents and purposes, single. I'm a naturally aggressive guy, I'm not bad-looking, and I've always liked to drink, smoke, and dance. I was in a job that brought me into contact with hundreds and hundreds of beautiful women. So I had a great time. I did it every day, and every night.

I usually woke up tired.

Through this period I wasn't divorced. I was only separated. It was in the early '80s that I separated from my wife for good, but it wasn't yet time for a divorce. That wasn't going to happen until Justin was grown. My wife wasn't surprised at my leaving. She was happy as long as I sent money each month to take care of her and my son. Since I wanted to do this, it was no problem. As I've said I didn't want to be the kind of father who didn't take care of his son. He was very important to me. Also, I didn't want him to grow up the same way I had, without a father. I made sure that didn't happen.

A NOTE ON DIVORCE: JAPANESE STYLE

Divorce has gotten more common among the Japanese, but not like in the States. A hundred years ago a Japanese man divorced his wife simply by writing her a note saying: "I don't want you to stay in this house anymore, so get out." Since then it's gotten a little more sophisticated. They've progressed to the point where marriages stay together until the children are grown. So even though a husband might go out whoring around every night, it's ok, as long as the wife stays home and brings the kids up.

People from other countries look at this and say: Look at how the Japanese women let the husbands go out and do all that—that's terrible. But those people don't understand. It's not terrible. What's bad is that the system is slipping. Western ways are coming in. There are good things in this. Women are freer to work, and hold responsible positions in a man's world. But now many families are falling apart. In the past the woman was appointed to be wife and mother only, both of which were positions of power and authority. The system dictated that they do that. Whether they wanted to do that, or not, the system said: yes. The nail that sticks out must be hammered down. Everybody did the same thing. So the wives, whatever they might've felt, did not react.

Now a lot of things have changed in more ways than one. Eight or nine years ago I was giving a lecture before a couple of dozen middle-aged Japanese women whose husbands were getting ready to retire.

After I was done a couple of them came up to me. Each one said something like: "I hate my husband. All he's worried about is getting the children raised, and I never see him. He's always out at the clubs drinking, and all that. In two years he's going to retire and get a big bonus, about $400,000. I'm going to take half of it, then divorce him." And I imagine that she did. The trend of Japanese women divorcing their husbands is quite new, and many people can hardly believe it.

Japanese women have become more Western, and as that has happened they have also become more demanding of their husbands. Japanese husbands however, are not always ready for the change.

I believe change is part of life, and boy did my life change a lot in Japan. One of those changes involved becoming a friend of a guy featured as the main character in "Tokyo Underworld" by author Robert Whiting. I'll talk about that story next.

10

On the Edge of Tokyo Underworld

Trying to get a grip on organized crime's vast power base is like emptying the sea with a teaspoon.

—Italian Government Prosecutor

When I first met Nick Zapetti I was looking for a job. He was setting up a deal to import chinchilla fur from Russia. Nick was always looking for an angle on something. He'd placed an ad in the newspaper looking for a quality control specialist. "Quality Control" was all it said, and that is what I'd done up until 1970. I saw the ad and decided to answer it.

I had another motive. I'd heard of Nick Zapetti, and wanted to meet him. I knew he was an Italian from Brooklyn, and I'd grown up among those people. I thought we might have some things in common.

I called him up that morning. We chatted for awhile, and set up a meeting. He'd been in the service during World War II, serving in the Pacific. He'd gotten out right after the war, and set up shop in Tokyo. He owned Nicola's, the first pizza restaurant the city had ever seen (it's still here, near a place called Izumi Gardens). It was famous among both the Japanese and the Americans, gradually gaining a reputation much like Nick's own. Gangsters liked to eat there. You could often see them coming and going.

In the 1950s and 1960s a lot of Italian guys from New York visited Tokyo. It was a natural thing. Some of them had been in the Pacific during the war, while others had been right there in Tokyo during the occupation. Still others were just curious. There was reason for curiosity. After the surrender, Japan lay in ruins, but it wasn't going to stay that way. When a nation is rebuilding from the ground up, there are always opportunities for a quick buck, and men who make a living on the wrong side of the law are always looking for that buck. These guys would go straight to Nick's place. It was a taste of home, and it was where they could find others like themselves who knew the ropes. Pretty soon any connected guy who came to Tokyo knew he should go see Nick.

Nick got involved in all kinds of things, and had developed quite a reputation as a kind of gangster over the years. I heard about those things, but I kept my participation pretty legitimate. Still we became friends, and I often ate at his restaurant.

I didn't get the quality control job. I knew quality control in communications systems, not chinchilla furs. I would guess that the only reason he talked to me was that I was from his old stomping grounds, and maybe he'd find some use for me eventually.

Nick was a colorful guy. He tried all kinds of businesses. If he could see an angle he'd take the chance. At one point he had a diary farm. He wanted to make his own cheeses for the pizzas he served. Another time he got into the sausage business. He had the same thought there, but in both ventures he was figuring on supplying more than just his restaurant. Nick had figured out early that there were a lot of creative ways to make some yen in Japan.

Most of Nick's reputation came from the years before I knew him. Coming to Tokyo in the '60s I'd seen a city where flimsy buildings were giving way to skyscrapers. The old Tokyo was a city of thin wooden houses subject to the whims of fire and quakes. When I first got here that still dominated, though it was giving way to the new. There was some money, and they'd started building, but it wasn't far along when compared to the way it is now. Today the only old wooden houses are around the shrines.

When I came here there were still whole sections of the city like that. When Nick arrived twenty-two years before me the old wooden architecture was all there was—that and huge expanses that had been leveled by American bombs. Nick's first view of Japan was of a beaten nation starting nearly a decade of occupation by a foreign power. Other cities, like the ones that had gotten the atomic bombs, were even worse off than Tokyo. Japan was destitute, and many of its people were on the verge of starvation. General McArthur had been appointed as a virtual dictator, heading the occupation. The rebuilding was starting, literally from the ground up, and an American like Nick could see angles around angles. It was: Anything goes.

By the time I knew Nick he was in his late fifties, and was suffering from diabetes. He was pretty fat by then. The man had eaten too much of his own food. Though he was slowing down, he hadn't run out of schemes, thus the chinchillas.

Nick had made huge amounts of money, but he'd spent almost all of it on women. He'd been married more times than I can count. All his wives were Japanese, and when he divorced one he always gave her a ton of money. I figured he spent over a million dollars for ex-wives when you include legal fees and other costs. That was how he made the break clean and final. Remember that these divorces were happening in the 1950s and 1960s, when a million bucks was a lot of money.

By the time I knew him he still had all the trappings of riches: a big house, big cars, and all the rest, but he was still a low-class guy. He was my friend, but I have to tell the truth about him. He had no education. He knew little of culture. He was just an Italian boy from New York making it big in Japan, and he never really made any effort to smooth off his rough edges. He was crude, had a bad temper, and he usually had the money to buy his way out of trouble.

But he also had a business—really several businesses that had succeeded in those first two decades. Japan was growing, and Nick had grown along with it. He used his shady reputation, cultivating connections with many people in that shadowy gray area between crime and legitimate business. He also knew how to take on the veneer of a gentleman when the moment required it. Once again, he knew the angles.

I knew a lot of American wheeler-dealers in my early years in Tokyo. They were a breed. Another who was more of my era was Danny Stein. He had a place called Danny's Inn, right across from the New Sanno Military Hotel in Hiro-o. He was an old New Yorker too. Danny had spent some time in Vietnam, and made a lot of money, but then he got sick, and needed to get out of there. Instead of heading back to the States, Danny came to Japan, and opened his club. He had a bunch of young Japanese prostitutes working for him there. They were in the club for the pleasure of the American servicemen staying in the hotel. Americans would go there on R&R, get all juiced up over in the hotel, then go across the street to Danny's. The young girls would take over from there, and Danny would make his money.

Danny became a close friend. When he moved his business around the corner I was a part of his club. He'd been in a large place called the James Lee building. Originally it had been owned by a suit company from Hong Kong. James Lee was the owner when Danny first opened, but Lee sold the building, and gave Danny a big chunk of money to move out. That's the system here. So Danny moved around the corner. I was part of the move. Once there Danny operated on the same system with the girls: they did their business, he got his cut.

A few years later I was sitting in the club with him, when the famous Mama, Maria, approached him. Maria had a place up in the Roppongi. She had mostly foreign girls. The police hadn't liked her operation there, so they told her to close it down. She said to Danny: "Listen, I'd like to buy half your place."

Danny asked: "Why?"

"I need a place for my girls to stay," Maria said.

Danny said: "Ok. Give me forty million yen."

Within a few days the lawyers had drawn up the papers, and Mama Maria walked into the club with a brown paper bag. The bag was full of yen—cold cash. She put it on the table, signed the papers, and from

then on she was half owner of Danny's Inn. That night twenty-five foreign prostitutes and a couple of gay boys started working the crowds
there.

The entertainment at Danny's was the girls. When a customer came
in not a minute would pass before he'd have his eye on a girl, or a girl
would have her eye on him. Either way, she'd grab him fast, sit him at
a table, and the waiter would come over. The girl would usually order
Johnny Walker Black, and the guy would do the same. There went
3,000 yen. At that point she'd whisper in his ear. They'd get up, leave,
and go to the Shanty Hotel, which was a ten-minute walk. They never
did drink the booze, so we'd pour that back in the bottle. We'd take six
months to go through a bottle of that stuff, and most of what we lost
was through spillage.

The Shanty was a fine hotel shaped like a castle. It was what the Japanese call a Love Hotel. These are hotels that are set up for getting laid.
You can use it all night, or just for a couple of hours, and many have
special afternoon prices for people who want a quickie. Japan still to
this day is filled with Love Hotels and although prostitutes still use
them, their business is mostly with young couples.

The girls would finish a job in as little as twenty minutes, and be
right back to the club to snag another. The girls made great money, but
they often sent home the lion's share of it. There were all national-
ities, French, American, Italian, Korean, Spanish, and one big blonde
gay boy who'd had a couple of operations…but they hadn't been able
to do anything about her Adam's apple. She'd sit around with the
other girls, and tell stories like this: "Oh, let me tell you, I had a guy
last night, and we get to the hotel, and he wants me to pull down my
panties and show it to him…and I do it…and he comes right away. I'll
tell you, I didn't even do anything. The next thing I know he's handing my 30,000 yen." Those kinds of things happened all the time with
her. For some reason her guys just couldn't control themselves.

It was a wild business, but I guess anyone could tire of it eventually. After a few years around the corner Danny left Japan and went to Las Vegas. There he opened the Las Vegas Trade & Travel Office. It was a service to book tourists into hotels when they arrived at the airport. Danny aimed it at Japanese tourists. Like a lot of men who go into business in Vegas, Danny fell into in the wrong scheme with the wrong woman. He wound up getting robbed, and beaten badly in the deal.

Danny left the club in my hands. I ran it with Maria for awhile. She was a German blonde, and pretty impressive. She and I would sit down at the end of each week, and divide up the proceeds. There would be all these little brown envelopes, and we would divide them up, one-for-you-one-for-me. If there was five yen left over she'd grab it and say: "That's mine." But by the same token, if I were to say: "Maria, I need a Rolex watch," she'd go and buy me one.

Running that club took a lot of long hours, but it was fun. I was always amazed at the people I saw in there. Tokyo's elite could often be found standing at the bar at Danny's.

But in the end I found that I wasn't really cut out for that kind of business. The police in Akasaka would always be coming to me and saying: "Keep the girls inside, Rick-san. They can't stand out in the street and sell it." We got along, but I knew it was only a matter of time before some kind of pressure would be brought to bear, and there I'd be with a police record as the owner of a whore house. That could've jeopardized my ability to stay in Japan, so I decided to get out of the business. I eventually sold my end to a gay boy from Korea, and sent Danny half the proceeds.

Not long before I met him Nick Zapetti had lost virtually everything. It was sad to see him that far down, though I'm sure there were plenty of people who were happy about it. I had no reason to be. At that point, Nick hadn't done anything to me. But he'd thrown away money, and trusted the wrong people, and now his fortune was shot. He'd lost his houses, his restaurant, his share in a cab company, and everything else. He claimed his creditors had stolen his personal stamp—his "hanko" which is used to sign legal documents—an important part of a foreigner's identity which allows the bearer to take possession of all property and money owned by the person to whom the stamp was issued. He sued, and kept it in court for years, opening up another restaurant in the meantime. It was about that time that he went back to the beginning of the line, and remarried his first wife, Yae Koizumi. She was very smart and clever, and she helped him regain some of what he'd lost. While he was with her he finally became a Japanese citizen. This helped him hang on to some of his holdings. Yae also helped him in a transition to a more natural lifestyle. Nick needed that. He was fast becoming a very sick man.

When I knew him he went from the chinchilla furs to a pig farm to other ventures that didn't go much of anywhere, but his wife knew enough to invest most of their money in department stores and other more solid projects. As the years passed he got sicker and sicker. I used to have to lead him out of the restaurant and guide him to the car where his wife was at the wheel. Nick couldn't drive because he could hardly see. His back bothered him from all the crap he'd been eating for so many years, and all the extra weight it produced. This was a guy who'd been physically formidable well into late middle age. Nick aged before my eyes.

Often I took care of him, and he was always saying: "Rick, could you help me with this…" I always did. Nick wasn't perfect, but he'd been decent to me and to other friends. Besides, you hate to see that happen to anyone.

Then came a time when Nick decided he couldn't handle the restaurant anymore. At that point he was still up and around, but barely. A friend of mine had an Indian restaurant, and he was planning to expand. Acting as agent in a business arrangement with Nick, I put together a deal with the guy, and had them meet. I brokered a deal where Nick would sell it to my friend for a million bucks. They reached agreement on details. I was in line for a finder's fee of three percent.

At that point my uncle died, which meant I had to drop everything and head back to the States. I was the nearest relative who was in a position to do what was necessary. I flew to New York, and handled the details. I had to be away for a month. That was fine. I'd put together the deal for Nick. All they had to do was sign the papers. I got back, and the restaurant had changed hands. I went back Nick's office, and told him I was glad the deal had gone through, then asked for my percentage.

Nick looked at me and said: "Well, Rick, you didn't really do much on that deal. When we were doing the actual business, and signing the papers you were off in the States."

I said: "What are you talking about? I found the guy, and put together the deal, and all you had to do was put your signature on a piece of paper."

"You didn't do enough to rate a fee," he said.

I slammed out of there. Two weeks later he went into the hospital and died.

I went to the wake. I was still upset. I figured Nick's wife owed me three million yen. So I said to her: "Yae, Nick died owing me three million yen."

She answered: "He owed it to you. I didn't owe it to you."

I said: "Look, the company owes it to me."

"No," she said. "That was between you and Nick. I don't owe it to you, and the company doesn't owe it to you." Then she asked: "Are you coming to the funeral?"

I said. "Since he owes it to me, I owe it to him to come and piss on his grave." I turned around and walked out, and never saw Yae Koizumi again.

Robert Whiting has written an excellent book about that whole era, centering around Nick's career. It's called "Tokyo Underworld" and he used me as one of his main sources. It details the various scams Nick was a part of, as well as many other illicit activities, including the Great Imperial Hotel jewelry heist, which Nick played a role in. Much of it was stuff I heard rumors about. I didn't have first hand knowledge of most of it. What I was able to do was point Robert in the right direction so he could find all the parts of the story. He turned his investigations into a compelling overview of organized crime in Tokyo since the end of World War Two.

Robert included a photo of me in the book. In it I'm standing in front of a club called One-Eyed Jacks. This is a club that became famous throughout the world. In the old days you went inside, then downstairs. If you stop there today you can see a picture of two pretty girls hanging on a wall there. I used to help them as their International Manager. Those are two of Japan's most famous women, the Kano Sisters.

To your right was a topless club, with fifty or so foreign women. Then in the back were Japanese women for guys who spoke no English. To the left was a casino. Gambling was illegal in Tokyo, but they got around that by operating in chips. You would cash your chips in for a paper receipt. You took that around the corner, and there they paid you whatever was shown on the receipt.

That closed down, and reopened as a strip place. It's still there.

One thing Whiting mentioned in his book was my involvement in 1985 in a short term project called the Bob Hope Golf Club. I didn't know it at the time, but there was a shady side to this scheme. It was run by a guy named Yamada.

They were going to build it at Iberaki, on a former dairy farm. In Japan this kind of deal is usually done by soliciting people to buy memberships to raise the money for the actual club, course, and grounds. Then the members would have equity in the place. We did sell memberships, but little was actually being built. There were huge problems. The biggest of these was that the farmers right at the center of the golf course had refused to sell. They were still there, and they weren't moving. But I'm not sure Yamada and the other people behind the scam even cared about that. I wound up thinking that they just intended to pocket the membership fees.

The people behind this paid Bob Hope for the use of his name, and even managed to get him to fly to Japan and publicly give it his blessing. Hope had no idea. They had a great reception for him, and later they even began digging a few holes.

But the scam slowly became obvious, even to those of us who worked on it. I was Executive Marketing Director, and I had to hire and train a staff to sell the memberships. But just as my sales team and I were going into high gear, this Japanese magazine started poking around, and found that Yamada had also been behind a Jack Nicklaus golf club earlier in the 1980s. There too, using a famous name, he'd fleeced a whole crowd of people. Fortunately we found out a little earlier in the process.

When dealing with such people there is always a price. As we were winding up this debacle, and it looked more and more like Yamada wouldn't pay, I had a phone number, and that got me in touch with a fellow I knew—a pretty good guy—whose position in his "organization" was "vice director". He sent one of his men to help me collect. With the vice director's man I was able to get the money back for the ones we'd sold. Once I had it I reimbursed our customers. Then at the end Yamada didn't want to pay me my fee. Because I had a few friends in the underworld I was finally able to get my money out of him. He'd done his best to stiff me. It wasn't until my friends intervened, and had some gentle talks with the people running the scheme, that Yamada came up with what he owed me.

But in the end no legitimate people I dealt with lost money. I was proud to say that I got myself and my customers out clean.

Once I had the money, I knew enough to take out my friend, the vice director and show him a good time. I blew half my fee on that. I didn't mind. My customers were happy, and I was obligated. That's the system. I knew the rules.

Cash Flow and the Tokyo Underworld

There was a point in the 1980s when I started spending more than I was making. It wasn't that I was doing badly. I wasn't. Money was coming in, but not as much as I was used to. But I was supporting my wife, sending my son to a good school, and living a lifestyle that required plenty of cash. I was the entertainer, the one who bought the guys drinks in Roppongi. I took the girls out to dinner. I entertained clients, and bigwigs of all stripes. I was known for it. It had become a part of my "face." In Japan keeping your "face" is very important. Without it no one will know you. It will soon be clear that you have no money and no support. You will be like the injured shark. The other sharks will feast on what's left, and you will entirely disappear from the scene. Then they might say: "What happened to Roa?" And no one will bother to answer. I couldn't take that chance.

So even though times were tough for me, I did my best to continue living the same way. I wasn't broke, but I did have negative cash flow. The only way I could keep up appearances was to continue doing what I was doing.

In Japan, as in most other places, there are several places to get money. One can go to friends, or one might go to a bank for a loan. Next there are the loan companies, but their interest rates are much higher. Then, outside the law, there are the loan sharks.

Now I'd made a lot of Japanese friends, some of whom were involved in these shadier financial areas. At one point I borrowed money from a guy I shouldn't have. You can imagine the interest rates. This was no by-the-month stuff; it was by-the-day. I wondered how I was going to get out of it. But luckily I had other friends who were able to come to my rescue. These friends lent me money to pay him off, and they weren't the type to break bones. The loan sharks had been ready to beat the shit out of me.

That was what they usually did. If for some reason they didn't want to beat you up they would come and sit in the waiting room of your office. They wouldn't do anything to you, but they'd scare the hell out of your clients, acting obnoxious, and making it clear that you were targeted. After a few days word would get around, and your business would dry up. At that point most people paid.

It was important to me to keep those kinds of vague accounts straight. There'd been too many times when those friends had asked me to help in their questionable activities. As long as we were already even, I could say: "No, thanks," and they wouldn't lean on me. That was how it worked.

These guys were all over Roppongi, and still are today. They are there every day, collecting protection money, doing business in the hostess clubs...occasionally they cross the line into extortion, but this is just the nature of the criminal element. To their credit, for many years they stayed away from the drug business. That isn't as true anymore, but it was then. In fact, the Yakuza (the term used for the Japanese Mafia) were a big part in helping Japan to grow. They kept the crazies off the streets, often better than the law did. They didn't kill people or rob banks. They had their own society and their own way of doing things. Hell, during the recent Kobe earthquake they were the first ones to help the people, long before the local government got their act together.

Now I tell the young guys: one of the biggest secrets of success is the people around you. You're only as good as they are. If you make good friends, and hire good people for your business, they'll get you through the hard times. After all, we're all in this together. We'll only make it by helping each other. I always tell them they can call me. If I don't have money I'll try to help in other ways. I've always got plenty of advice. I'll always answer your call. Then I lean toward them, and tell them: "And if I call you, you better answer my call." Of course, when I say that, they look at me and say: "Ah, Roa, our guy from Brooklyn, we love the way you talk."

Sometimes they think I'm joking.

Korea 1953, Roa ready for action.

17 year old Rick Roa.

My grandmother, great grandmother, and me the blondie.

The Kano Sisters (on my sides) and my assistant Yuki.

Matsuoka, retired Japanese Tennis Great,
and now Japanese TV personality.

The Playboy Millennium 2000 twins in Tokyo.

Devi Sakarno, former wife of the Indonesian President, and now a
famous TV personality, & Sal Savino, a good friend.

Great Boss: The late great IMG Chairman Mark McCormack and Zen
Shirai, visionary Chairman of Japan Rugby Football Union.

My son Justin at my wedding reception, does that sound strange?

The American Train in Japan Operating Committee,
with the President of the Ritz Hotel Group.

The Hustler in Roppongi.

One of the happiest days of my life,
Machiko and me at our wedding reception.

A man for all seasons, my friend M. Ishihara.

Steve Miller,
President & CEO of the Professional Bowling Association.

Me on the stage at the famous Budokan Hall with the hit Japanese
music group, Alfee's.

Knighted with my old and trusted friend, Seigen Toriyama.

Christine Hefner (center) and Kano Sisters (sides) at the opening of
the Playboy Boutique in Japan 2002.

Former Prime Minister Mori-san, a lover of Rugby.

The great Jesse, former Sumo star (center), Sir John Ackhurst, Governor General of the Board of Governors, Harrow School, England (wearing glasses), and the Bursar of Harrow School, Michael Liddiard.

Roger Utley visiting Tokyo. Former great Rugby Player and coach of the Harrow School rugby team.

Rick and Matt Kass for the Japan Professional Bowling Association
(JPBA).

Rick Roa with author and friend, Tony Teora.

11

Becoming an Organizer and Promoter: The Great American Train

Nothing is impossible; there are ways that lead to everything, and if we had sufficient will we should always have sufficient means. It is often merely for an excuse that we say things are impossible.

—François de La Rochefoucauld

When the Bubble started I was already in business for myself, wheeling-and-dealing, mostly promoting things. That was why I'd been approached to do the Bob Hope Golf Club project. They wanted someone who could do the job. Most of my clients were nothing like Yamada, and I'd won myself a reputation as a straightforward guy.

When you're a maverick you'd better be honest. After all, when you're asking people to deal with something unusual, you can't be lying to them.

By the mid-1980s the Bubble Time was in full swing, and anyone who was a wheeler-dealer was looking to get in on it. There was plenty of money around, and if you could think up a new and fascinating project people would back you. When I'd been in advertising I'd learned how to make something sell. Now I wanted to create new ways of selling things. Gradually I realized I could sell huge things: broad concepts and big ideas. I could even sell an entire nation's ideas and products to another nation. That was what the Great American Train was all about.

But I'm getting ahead of myself. I've written of my boy, Justin, and I should mention him here, because when we start doing the really big things in life, in some ways we're doing them for our kids. They are the ones who will follow us, and pick up the world we made for them. Will they have something worthwhile? That depends on us.

My son Justin was born in 1971. I'd been home with him a lot at first, but as the years passed, and I grew apart from my wife, I wasn't home as often. By the early 1980s I was living in Tokyo full time. I made sure I still saw him, and provided for him, and had an influence on him. I worked to be a good father.

Through most of these years he was going to school and growing up in the Japanese system of society. When he was in the early grades he joined the Little League, which is quite big here in Japan. Justin developed into an excellent ballplayer. His teammates and coaches accepted him easily, even though he was of mixed blood. I went to many of his games. I made a point of it. I would go and watch from the sidelines. As I watched him become a star I was incredibly proud. He won trophies and awards right and left, enough to fill a cabinet.

Justin knew his father was different. I wanted him to be raised in the Japanese System, but I also wanted him to be aware of his American heritage. Maybe he understood it best simply in knowing that I was not the same as the other fathers. His friends' fathers were perfectly good men, and provided well for their boys. They cared as deeply for their sons as I did for mine. But they were also Japanese salarymen. They worked for large companies, and fit in. They didn't stick out, so they never had to be hammered down.

In my own country the example that would be most like a Japanese business would be IBM. In the 1950s and 1960s there was no American corporation that better reflected the idea of conformity. Men who worked for IBM wore white shirts, button-down collars, and ties of designated color and width. Black suits and oxfords were standard. They kept their desks neat, and used standard forms for every memo and letter. They all answered their phones the same way, and, most importantly, they all thought the same way.

That last part is the key. IBM might have easily taken the Japanese mantra: The nail that sticks out must be hammered down. Those guys at IBM never stuck out. If their heads rose even slightly above the wood they never got hired in the first place.

In Japan all the companies were like that. That was how Japan had gotten ahead. They were a society accustomed to obedience. They were as fierce about fitting in as Americans are about being individuals. In America there can only be so many IBMs. In Japan there could be only so many mavericks.

Maybe my Japanese associates could take the idea of being different a little more easily if it came from their American friend, Rick-san. After all, I wasn't disrespectful. I had (and have) a deep respect for the Japanese way of life. But I approached their system as any boy from Brooklyn would. I looked for the angles.

Justin took a lot of pride in having a maverick father. While most of the fathers he saw did everything society expected of them, Justin knew his dad was the nail that stuck out. They kept trying to hammer me down, but I wouldn't be hammered. I was on my own doing interesting things. I was enjoying life, and I was helping them enjoy their lives. Justin may not have understood all of this, but he knew it instinctively. It felt great to have a son who was as proud of me as I was of him.

Justin is doing quite well in the Japanese world. I am glad that he is, because I knew it was the world he'd been born into. I made sure he went to good schools, and fit in well with the Japanese system. But I also encouraged him to always have his own thoughts.

As my son grew up, I was living in a community of Japanese and Americans. The Japanese among us dared to be a little different from their compatriots, if only in that they would allow foreigners into their ventures. And as for us Americans—well, what can I say—we were Americans. All of us were wheeling and dealing. I was often a conduit between American and Japanese concerns.

It was because of this that my focus accidentally shifted into promoting events. The most fateful part of that shift came when my friend, Fred Daté asked me if I wanted to go to a seminar on finding new ideas to promote the East Japan railroad.

It was 1987 and the Japanese Government, which had owned all the railroads lock, stock, and train track, had just split the system. At the heart of the split up was Japan Railways Group, know as JR. JR was a government-subsidized group of eight companies that took over most of the assets, operations, and liabilities of the government-owned Japanese National Railways in 1987. At first the companies remained in the public domain, but privatization began for some of the companies later on in the 90's. One of those companies was the East Japan Railroad.

As private companies will, the East Japan Railroad was looking to attract more customers. They wanted to show the people that the East Japan railroad was the choice for freight and riders. Now that people had some choice they had to.

The idea fueling the seminar was that the East Japan Railroad should enter the ring fighting, and stage a big event to announce its new look. They had decided that this should be so, but no one had the slightest idea of what kind of event it ought to be.

I wasn't ignorant of events. I'd worked on plenty of projects in Tokyo where some big happening was the centerpiece of a promotional campaign. There would be parties, openings—possibly even a prolonged campaign of such happenings. I'd worked on many of these, but it was always a part of something else: an advertising campaign, or a business opening. I'd never really thought of doing coordination of an event as the subject of a promotional campaign, but it wasn't so difficult a leap.

The company in charge of getting something done was Nihon Kotsu Bunka Kyokai. They had worked on a lot of the billboard and sign advertising for the old Japanese Railroad. Nihon Kotsu Bunka Kyokai sent their people around to try to get the best ideas they could for such an event. Thus came the seminar, and my presence, and ultimately my participation. I sat and listened to others talk. I heard ideas, and more ideas. I turned things over in my mind. I thought of trains. I thought of Japanese trains—a truly excellent system at its core. I thought of my own country, and its systems, which reminded me of the huge trade deficit the U.S. was running with Japan.

At some point someone asked me what I thought. I said: "Just off the top of my head, why not try to do something for the Japanese trade problem with the United States." Everyone looked at me. Here was the nail-sticking-out talking. I couldn't figure out what else to do but say what I thought: "So why don't we have a train that promotes American products." They nodded, as the Japanese will, and kept talking. The idea of a train promoting American products didn't hold up as the subject under discussion.

I left there figuring I was just out cab fare. I'd put in my two cents. I hadn't expected any more than that. After all, we go to a lot of meetings in this life, and only a few end up mattering.

But a couple of weeks later my friend called me up. "Hey, Rick, the railroad people were very interested in what you said. They'd like to meet with you."

"Really?" I asked.

"Really," he said. "One of the owners wants to talk with you. He'd like to know about your idea with a little more definition. Can you do that?"

"Sure," I said. In truth I was shocked. I'd been serious at the seminar, but when no one else picked up on it, I figured it was time to go on to the next thing. Now this guy wanted to meet with me.

So a few days later I met with Mr. Taki, the President of Nihon Kotsu Bunka Kyokai. I knew what I was going to say when I sat down, and I said it: "You should have a train called 'The American Train in Japan.' The whole train should promote American products that are available here. Those products should be sold on the train. More than that, those products should *be* the train. They should be the entire interior, and the exterior should tell about them, and about the train as a whole. The train promotes the products, and the products promote the train."

Mr. Taki nodded, and said: "That's it. That's what we were looking for."

A few weeks later I went up there and signed a contract. I was going to work for them for the length of the project. They were willing to go with the Maverick, and the Maverick was there.

Then Mr. Taki showed me my new office. He opened the door, and there was this room where you could've fit about two hundred people—but it was absolutely bare. There might've been a desk or two and a couple of chairs, but in all the cubic footage a few sticks of office furniture were barely visible.

"This is your office, Roa-san."

I laughed, and said: "Well, Mr. Taki, the first thing I need is a secretary."

How I got my secretary is a story in itself. In a pure coincidence, about two weeks before (I had no thought of the train project at that point, it having been a single meeting where nothing much had seemed to happen) I met a Japanese-American woman, Jeanie. She was working as a sales clerk in the Washington Shoe Store in the Ginza. She was an attractive girl.

As she was helping me shop, I asked her if she liked her work.

"Are you kidding?" she asked. "I'm only doing this because I have to work for a living. It doesn't pay much, and I'm always looking for something else. I can do secretarial work."

"Well," I said, "If I ever have anything I'll come and find you."

Neither Jeanie nor I thought too seriously about my offer. I did mean it. She seemed to be a competent girl, and she got along with people, two qualities you'd want in any secretary. But I didn't have anything open right at that moment, and I said so. But three weeks later there I was, back in the shoe store.

She looked up, and smiled. Maybe she had some inkling of what I was about to say. After all, why else would I be back?

"Jeanie," I told her, "quit this job today, because tomorrow you're going to put those secretarial skills to work—for me."

She was blown away. "You really have a job for me?"

"I have a job, and it's a good one," I said. "The pay is good, and the project is a big one. We're going to put together a whole train full of products from American companies. It's going to be a showcase, and it's going to go everywhere there is to go in the country. You're going to love it."

"I will," she said.

The next morning there she was. She was surprised at the whole situation. So was I. But I wasn't wrong about Jeanie. She turned out to be just as good a secretary as I thought she'd be. She was efficient, and learned quickly, and she was very good with people. Over the next months all of those qualities would be put to the test.

Jeanie was my first hire. When she first saw the office it was in almost the same condition as it had been when I had walked in two days before. Maybe we had another stick or two of office furniture, but basically the huge room was still empty. Together we began to put things together. Phones arrived. We brought in typewriters and terminals, and desks to set them on. As the chairs came in the door, so did the people. I had a staff to hire. I talked to them, and Jeanie looked them over too. She was, after all, the senior staffer.

The job ahead was huge. When everything was decided they handed us an eleven-car train. Inside and out it looked like any line of train cars. There were seats, and areas for storage. Little of what was there was any good to us.

We tore out everything from the interiors, stripping the cars to the bone. We had work crews, supervisors, and those of us from the office. We were busy trying to figure out how we would fill all this space.

Early on I brought in the official brass of my own home country. I teamed up with the American Embassy. I knew the people there well enough. I'd been to their parties for years, and I saw America's diplomatic elite at parties at other embassies. So I brought them in to help line up American companies, giving the train a quasi-official cast. Through the Embassy we got the US Department of Commerce involved. They were happy as hell to see something like this happening. It was US policy to encourage the sale of more American products in Japan, and our train was going to be the great symbol of that effort. We painted the train red, white, and blue, and painted big stars on it. On the front we put the bald eagle. This train was going to be American in more than just name. It was going to be a commercial emissary to the people of Japan.

By this time I had about forty people working for me. They'd worked themselves to the bone, and their efforts were paying off. We were finally ready to do a formal presentation to an audience of company representatives.

Being boss of this whole enterprise, and Marketing Director for the train, the presentation was mine to make. Jeanie and the others helped with all the preparations, then came the day when I appeared before my fellow Americans and told them how this opportunity would work. They could see the cars, all clean, stripped, and ready for displays and sales. I gave them a program. We would have the train for a year. It would be a year like no other for these companies. Their best face would roll through Japan in a huge display of American quality. This would put every product forward in its best light. It would be a whole new way of reaching the Japanese market. Japan's consumers would be thrilled, and its businessmen couldn't help but be impressed.

I could see the interest build. After the initial presentations I met with the representatives of the various companies. We solidified the timetable. The train would leave from Tokyo, and go all over Japan. We would start on America's birthday, the Fourth of July, 1988.

Each car would be occupied by a single company. On the outside, along with all our flourishes, was the company logo. Inside the car the company would display its products. There would be service people selling American products, making presentations, and answering any and all questions. All service would come with a smile. Companies handpicked their people for this venture. It was a commercial and diplomatic undertaking that would eventually cost over seventy million dollars.

Soon I found myself crossing the Pacific. There I was back in my home country selling my fellow Americans on this venture in international trade. For instance, I'd begun here in Tokyo with Coca-Cola. They thought it was interesting but said: "It's really too expensive for us. The whole thing is just so...big!" I knew that was what made the project great, and I wasn't satisfied with their answer. Coca-Cola is a huge concern in Japan, and I wanted them and all their products to be on the train.

So when I went to the States my first stop was Atlanta, Georgia where Coca-Cola is headquartered. I walked in cold, with no introductions or scheduled meetings. I figured I might do best if I took them by surprise. After all, The Train was an incredibly surprising undertaking. In no time I found myself in the office of the Global Marketing Director. I told him exactly what we were doing, and why.

"I went to Coca-Cola in Tokyo," I said.

"What did they tell you?" he asked.

"They didn't seem to be ready for something like this," I said.

He shook his head. "Maybe they just weren't used to this kind of approach."

"Maybe," I said. "But America is a big country. Americans like me go out into the rest of the world, and play a role like no other. I got this thing going because a Japanese railroad president recognized that. I don't understand why Coca-Cola, one of our greatest companies, wouldn't see it too."

"You're right, of course," he said. "It must be some kind of ridiculous misunderstanding. Maybe they just need to know how the people here in America feel. Where are you staying, Mr. Roa?"

"The Ritz-Carlton," I said.

"I'll call you," he said.

I went back to my hotel room, and the next thing I knew he was on the phone. "When you get back to Japan our people will be waiting for you," he said. "You just tell them what you need."

It really was that simple.

That was how the trip went. My colleagues and I approached the business people in my own country and the idea of the Train began to take hold. It was a whirlwind tour through Georgia, Florida, and other states, and it left all of us a little crazy.

When we got to New York on New Year's Eve we were all a little worn down. The Japanese guys I was with included Mr. Taki, and my good friend Sekiguchi, who you'll hear more about in awhile. Those guys wanted to go out somewhere fancy and get the best meal money could buy, meaning the most expensive. I knew my old home town, and knew what the best thing to eat would be: a huge pastrami sandwich on a soft roll, cole slaw, potato salad and a kosher pickle. They were bent on going to a high-priced French place, and I had the hardest time explaining to them that all I wanted was a true New York delicatessen meal. Funny how people never listen to the wisdom of a native.

At the New Ontani Hotel in Los Angeles Taki had decided he wanted something American to wear. He picked up a big cowboy hat. Now Taki was built like a typical Japanese guy of his generation: he was pretty small. In addition he wore big glasses. When he put on this ten-gallon hat it seemed to swallow him up. He pushed it back enough to see, which gave us a view of Taki looking absolutely tiny. His glasses seemed as big as he was. The hat seemed several times larger. Taki wore his John Wayne hat as if it were a crown. He would rule on where we would go, and where we would eat. He dismissed my idea about deli food, and dragged all of us into a Chinese restaurant. As they brought us food and drink, Taki sat there sweating. He'd taken off his jacket, and was down to a sweat-stained white shirt. His glasses were like big reflectors. They shone from above his buck-toothed smile, and they were topped by that crazy hat. After enough food and drink (emphasizing the drink) Taki opened his shirt down to his belly button, hopped up, and sat cross-legged on the chair, as if he were sitting on the Japanese tatami mat in his own house. Sekiguchi and I, and the rest of our party all stared at him, not believing our eyes. Taki then proceeded to order a big bowl of noodles. When they got there he dove in, slurping the noodles so everybody in the place could hear. I mean, he was slurping loud, like a Japanese man might do behind the closed door of his own home.

I looked around, and realized our friend was center stage. The whole place was looking at him. Most of them didn't seem offended. He was just a curiosity. Sekiguchi and I, and our colleagues had brought in this weird Japanese guy for the Americans to look at. Taki was the show.

That's Americans for you. We're always ready for a carnival, and what we like most is the sideshow acts: we're easily entertained.

And Taki was certainly entertaining.

That was a Japanese millionaire being himself in the Land of the Free.

Our trip took on a successful aura, though maybe not because of our off-hours behavior. Once we had Coca-Cola the rest fell into place. Now it began to look like the enterprise I had planned all along. Coca-Cola, American Express, and all the other companies put together exhibitions to sell their products right from the train. These were companies that might be famous for one particular product (a soft drink, or a credit card), but they all had many different brand names under their umbrellas. Coca-Cola had Minute Maid orange juice. AmEx showed off all their various financial services. The point wasn't just to sell cola; it was to show the Japanese people what kinds of companies these were. So in the train car they'd have exhibitions, movies, and a place where you could actually buy the products. Each car was unique. It was like a traveling fair with the best exhibits anyone had ever seen.

Never had America had such an exhibition in Japan. Outgoing Prime Minister Nakasone became our honorary chairman. When the new prime minister was about to go to the U.S. Nakasone told him: "Make sure there's a blurb in your speech for this." Sure enough, when the prime minister spoke at Union Station in Washington, he said: "Japan is trying to do her best to ease trade relations with the United States, and we are proving this with the American Train in Japan." I was there in the audience, and I heard him say it.

Opening day was July 4th, 1988, just as we'd planned. There were no hold-ups or major glitches. We'd done the spadework for this project, selling where the selling was tough, and setting the right tone throughout. America was well-served here.

Miss American Train presided over the opening, along with her consorts. They'd all been selected from contestants in Hawaii. They were a beautiful group of girls. We had the station masters all dressed in white. All the major members of the government were there, as was a big American ribbon. Our transportation minister at that time was a famous writer, Ishihara (he's now the Governor of Tokyo). He cut the ribbon. The train's first stop was in the Emperor's private station. This was a station once reserved only for those trains that would carry the royal family. Even now it was not an everyday stop. It was there that we had the first real show. CBS and NBC had their cameras on hand for the ceremonies. Of course, there in Japan it was front page news.

Once the train was underway the hardest part of my work was over. I stayed with the train at the start, but I also knew better than some people when to get off. I had done what was necessary and a whole lot more. I would still keep an eye on this project, which was, after all, my baby. But it was more than that. It was an expression of the commercial inventiveness of my whole country. I was more like the doctor who brought this baby into the world, helping two great nations understand each other better.

The Great American Train was a hit everywhere it went, and it went everywhere. Jeanie and all the rest of the staff had a great deal to be proud of.

◆   ◆   ◆

For a guy who had never done any major promotion for events, this was certainly a huge start. I had a blast doing it from start to finish. From then on they called me "Mr. American Train" around the American Embassy. It was humbling to be a part of such a great project for the American people. I was getting a great deal of attention, but who deserved it more? And now I was certain that I was ready to do my own thing. After all, this event business really seemed to agree with me. Little did I know how big this event business would become. In my next story I'll talk about how I brought the top music talent to Japan working with Dick Clark.

12

A Parade of Stars

Champions aren't made in gyms. Champions are made from something they have deep inside them—a desire, a dream, a vision. They have to have last-minute stamina, they have to be a little faster, they have to have the skill and the will. But the will must be stronger than the skill.

—Muhammad Ali

I should give you a proper introduction to my friend, Sekiguchi. He's an excellent writer, and does some of the best presentations in Japanese business. He's worked in politics, most prominently as campaign manager for the professional wrestler Inoki, who ran for the Japanese Diet. Inoki once wrestled with Muhammad Ali. His key phrase was "Sports for Peace." He ran his campaign out of a bowling alley next to the Tokyo Tower.

As Election Day edged closer Inoki started talking about making peace with Russia (this was in the '80s while the Cold War was still on). His slogan for this platform was "Sports for Peace."

Sekiguchi looked for a way for Inoki to capitalize on this slogan. He decided his candidate should get on television and talk about "Sports for Peace" with a Russian woman.

"But where am I going to find a Russian woman who can talk about this with Inoki?" he wondered.

"That's easy," I said. "I can get you one."

That night I made the rounds in Roppongi. Just as I knew I would, I found a Russian hostess. She was pretty and articulate in Japanese.

Hostesses can usually communicate pretty well. It's all that time they spend talking to men.

I said to her: "Do you want to be on TV?"

"Sure," she answered.

"Then come out to the Tokyo Tower bowling alley to be interviewed on TV tomorrow."

"Who's going to interview me?" she asked.

"A guy who's pretty important around here. Inoki."

As I expected, she was excited. Everyone knew who Inoki was, and to appear with him on television would be an honor. She arrived at the bowling alley the following day looking her best for the cameras. Inoki explained what Sports-For-Peace was, and asked her how she thought it might help ease the Cold War.

"Would this make relations better?" he asked.

She smiled, and replied: "It sounds as if it would relieve a great many tensions." Her Russian accent did the trick. No one ever knew that Inoki was talking to a hostess from a Roppongi club.

Inoki won. It was an election where the top few candidates were elected. He came in last among the winners, but he wound up serving for many years. He became a sort of goodwill ambassador for Japan, serving in the Diet, but also going to other countries to promote the Sports-For-Peace idea. He sometimes got into controversies, but all in all he did well. He quit a few years ago, and went back to wrestling. In the course of all that we became friends.

His campaign manager, Sekiguchi and I did many projects together. When we first decided we wanted to do the American Music Awards Concert series, we flew to Los Angeles, and had a meeting with the key people in Dick Clark's company, Dick Clark Productions (DCP). We'd had this huge idea about bringing a whole group of American superstars to Japan for a concert series. There's been nothing like it before. We envisioned a solid week of concerts, each bigger than the last. We contacted people in Dick Clark's company, and they seemed to like the idea. We'd faxed and had phone calls for several weeks, but each side was anxious to meet the other. We were certainly under the impression that they were serious about doing this with us, so we flew to L.A.

We drove to their headquarters our first day there. They ushered us into an office with a large round table. Fran LaMania, president of DCP, Elvira, their in-house lawyer, and their lead producer, Larry Klein were all there, but Sekiguchi and I kept looking for Dick Clark. We asked Fran where the big man was, and he told us Dick would be there in a few minutes.

Informally we began the meeting without him. The three of them asked us about some general things, and some particulars. Sekiguchi and I told them some details of what we wanted to do and how we would do it. We had a wish list, and we went through some of it, and in return we told them a little about the finances. We didn't hold anything back, but we were keeping our whole presentation in reserve for when the big man joined us.

Then in walked Dick. I was impressed. Remember, like so many Americans, I'd grown up watching this guy. When I was in Brooklyn he'd just started the American Bandstand. To me Dick Clark was, and is an icon. He'd been a giant in the worldwide entertainment industry for decades. In many ways he was an industry unto himself. He helped start rock n' roll, and he brought a lot of the best of it to a whole generation of us. So now there I was in the same room with the man. He came in, and sat down right next to me. I introduced myself. Although Dick impressed me I tried not to show it. After all, this was business.

He said: "I'm glad to meet you guys. I'm glad you came. I think it's important to hear anybody out. Now Fran LaMania has told me about the project. He is going to work with you guys, but to tell you the truth, I don't think you can do this. I don't think you've got the money." And with that he got up and left.

We were shocked. I looked at Fran and said: "Is he always like that?"

He said: "Well, we're talking about Dick Clark here. You guys just arrived, and you've got to remember, we get all kinds of propositions.

You're a first for us, and quite frankly I'm not sure how we're going to do this. It's going to cost a lot of money. And because I'm not sure, I haven't been able to completely sell Dick on the idea."

So I said: "Please let Dick know that we're for real here. We're serious, and we do have the money. We're willing to do whatever is necessary, within reason."

"Then let's move forward," Fran said.

This could have made for a rocky start. Some men wouldn't have asked any questions. They would've walked out. But I thought Dick was just testing things out. By putting things that way, he immediately put us on the spot, which was the only way for him to know for sure that we were for real. Dick was interested in partnerships, and huge international projects, but he wasn't interested in being left holding the bag. He was a businessman, and I respected that.

Dick Clark soon learned that we were for real. Mostly we dealt with Fran, but it was easy to see Dick's eye was on the situation. Soon he had evidence of our seriousness. Not long after we returned to Tokyo they called. Fran wanted a million dollars transferred to the States. "It's the licensing fee for the name," he said. To use The American Music Awards isn't cheap, I thought to myself, but to get the stars to do the deal we needed that name. We also needed Dick Clark. I said, "Give us a little time." With the help of my team we had it there instantly.

With that first million delivered, counted, and in the bank, they knew we were for real. At that point everything started moving on a faster track. Sekiguchi and I began traveling back and forth between L.A. and Tokyo every couple of weeks. We had sponsorships to line up, contracts to be signed, and schedules to juggle. I did most of this traveling. It made sense because I was working on a huge event at the Portland Rose Festival in Oregon at the time.

The next time I saw Dick was when Fran, Larry, and I were discussing which artists would participate. Dick's office is on the first floor, so as you come in the main door you pass his secretary. Dick's room is in the back, and he can look right through to see everyone who's coming and going. One day as I came in he waved at me, and said: "Come on in here." He was friendly that time.

Dick's office is decked out with pictures of every superstar you can imagine. He's got honorary keys to every town in America in there—and probably keys to every major city on Earth. Dick's fame precedes him, and he uses that, rather than letting himself be used by it. He's not the first smart businessman to say: "Where's the money?"

Now that we were past that issue life with Dick Clark was down-right pleasant. Plus, being connected to Dick Clark opened doors, a lot of them. I'll explain two major introductions that came through this project. The first was Stevie Wonder.

In 1990 Stevie Wonder was at the top of his career. You needed some major music connections and some real luck to get a chance to do a deal with Stevie Wonder, so when his manager contacted me at Dick Clark's office in Beverly Hills I was flabbergasted.

"Are you Mr. Roa from Tokyo?"

I said, "Yes, who are you?"

"I'm Stevie Wonder's manager, he would like to meet you Mr. Roa. Are you interested?"

I said almost out loud, "Why da fuck would Stevie Wonder want to speak to *me*?" I thought about this later and realized everyone in Beverly Hills knew I was connected to buckets of the Japanese bubble money. The stars wanted a piece of this, and word got around about the deal. The stories were all about Dick Clark and this strange American who was working with the Japanese. So I answered the manager, "Sure, I'd love to meet Stevie Wonder."

The next day this lady drove me down Santa Monica Boulevard until we came to this house that said, *The Wonder House.* I expected a Zoo or some extravagant house considering what I read about guys like that. I'd had just enough contact with superstars to expect something out of Loony Tunes. I was pleased to see that Stevie Wonder kept a somewhat conservative look to his place.

On entering the house the lady manager ushered me into a small private room where Stevie was busy turning dials, and fiddling with electronic controls. He looked just as I'd expected: dark sunglasses, hair braided and swept back. He sat on a kind of stool and looked pretty busy hitting a keyboard. I assumed he was working on some new music. I knew Stevie was blind, so I was a little amazed at how busy things were around his desk. There was enough organized chaos that most people could have kept track of it with two sets of sighted eyes. As I walked in the lady said, "Stevie, this is Mr.Roa, the gentleman doing the American Music concert series in Japan."

Stevie put out his hand and I reached over and shook it.

"It's great to have you out here, Mr. Roa."

"Please call me 'Rick,'" I said.

The lady left the room while Stevie fidgeted with some dial connected to a musical device. "Please call me 'Stevie' and take a seat. It's great to meet you Rick. So how do you like Japan?"

I sat down in a leather coach and looked up to where Stevie was working. "Love it. Been there over twenty years."

"I like it to," Stevie then gave a puzzled look. "Hey Rick, I'm having some trouble with the volume control, can you turn up the volume over there for me?"

I started to think: This guy is really obsessed with music. I guess I should've expected that. Obsessions could be about a lot worse things, so I was happy to help. "What dial?" I asked.

"It should be in front of you somewhere on the right, can you please push it up until I say stop?"

"Sure."

I never found out what Stevie was working on that day, but whatever it was I was honored to be a part of it. I pushed a few levers. Stevie looked pleased. I wondered if I'd just joined the ranks of record producer. Hey, some of the best work around goes uncredited, right?

"Good job, Rick—thanks." Stevie hit a few more keys and fidgeted with more electronic dials. A small child rushed into the room and jumped onto the coach next to me.

"Hello," he said.

I said hello back and then the child started to run around the room. He then jumped on Stevie who smiled. Stevie held him for a little bit and then the child ran out of the room.

Stevie smiled. "Children, aren't they beautiful?"

I said, "Yes, they sure are. I have a son."

"That's wonderful."

Stevie hit a few more buttons, then looked as if he was typing into something. It was hard to tell. This man never stopped being busy.

"So Rick, ya know I really enjoyed my last trip to Japan."

"That's great, you should come back again, I'm sure they'd love to have you back."

Stevie then clicked some switches. "Rick, can you move that second dial down a bit?" I had no idea what he was talking about, but I moved some dials.

Stevie said, "Thanks." He then hit a few more keys. It was definitely music. It seemed Stevie was trying to get some kind of tune the way he wanted it. He was focused on this while we talking. "Yeah, I like Japan. How is the weather now?"

"This time of the year in the fall it's nice, it's only the hot humid summers that I don't like."

"California has some of the best weather in the world."

"I agree, and some of the nicest homes."

Stevie stopped hitting music keys. "Would you like to see my house Rick? It's not much but I have this great studio."

"I'd love to check it out."

Stevie then walked me around. Though his house was not flamboyant, the neighborhood could not have been more exclusive.

He took me into his home studio. It was a room where he and other people must have made music. It had a stage and looked very practical.

"You make your music here?" I asked.

"Sometimes."

Stevie and I then we spoke about the music industry in Japan and my promotion business. Before I left I wanted something to remember him by, a souvenir of an incredibly interesting afternoon, but I was hesitant.

"Stevie, I'm a little embarrassed but would you *mind* giving me your signature?"

"Of course Rick, it'd be my pleasure. I'll give you a picture that has my personal autograph."

Stevie called in a lady and asked for one of his signed pictures, he told the lady he wanted to do a personal signature. The lady brought in his picture and an inkpad. The picture was already signed. Stevie put his thumb print in the ink and then put it on the picture.

He gave one of his famous Stevie smiles. "Here Rick, now you have an authentic Stevie Wonder autograph."

I was happier than anyone could imagine.

As I was leaving Stevie spoke, "I really appreciate you coming and talking with me."

"It was *my* pleasure Mr. Wonder," I said.

It was only after I left that I realized Stevie had not hit me up for any type of promotional deal. Hell, I was bringing top stars to Japan. But, as I soon learned, Stevie left the business end up to other people. I would imagine that anyone who spent an hour or two with Stevie would automatically want to work with him, so the manager's job would be easy. That came in the ride back. Stevie's manager drove me, letting me enjoy the view of Santa Monica Boulevard.

"So Mr. Roa, did you have a good time with Stevie."

"He's a wonderful guy. We had a great time."

"He is a nice man, isn't he?" She then looked over at me and continued, "Did you know he is going to do a final tour?"

I thought to myself: final tour? Is he really going to retire? I'd seen a bunch of musicians do so-called "final tours" that weren't really final at all.

"No, I didn't," I said.

"It's going to be a very big worldwide final tour."

Ok, even if it wasn't really what the words said, I knew any world-wide tour by Stevie Wonder would be a big event. "Wow, I didn't know that. Stevie didn't mention that."

The lady smiled. "Yeah, he's even considering doing a couple concerts in Japan. We could set up the last two concerts in Japan as the final goodbye from Stevie Wonder, the last one be the final sayonara."

I now knew where this was leading. "Well, I'd love to organize that if that's something you're interested in doing."

The lady smiled. "We're looking for a *global* sponsor, Mr. Roa, not just a sponsor for Japan. We need someone to sponsor this global tour. If you had someone in Japan that could do the entire world concert series I think we could make sure that the last two concerts—the final concerts—were in Japan."

"I'd be interested in talking to my people in Japan about this. They might be interested."

"That's great Rick, if you think *you* can do it."

I knew I'd hit the sweet spot of the discussion. I knew Stevie would not be cheap so I was careful with my next question.

"You just tell me how much it will *reasonably* take and I'll talk to my people in Japan. But no promises."

The lady turned her head and looked at me as we stopped at a light. "Forty million."

I was shocked. I knew Stevie was expensive but *holy shit!* As a promoter I knew to keep my cool. "*Forty million dollars to do the concert?*" I asked.

"Yeah, I think that's the lowest we could do the deal."

I knew a final tour would be a big job, and if we could sponsor it from Japan my cut would be real sweet, but this amount of money meant big risk for one star. Even for a star like Stevie Wonder this was a lot of fucking money. You had to gross enough globally for people to make money beyond the forty million.

"I will talk to my people in Japan and if they can make money on this deal for the concert series I'm sure they'll be interested. I'll get back to you."

The lady crossed the intersection. "Forty million just for Stevie. They'll have to pay whatever it takes to cover the band and other expenses."

I though *fuck! This* is *gonna be impossible!* This is one hell of an expensive guy. I couldn't make sense of it. "If you could please fax over the best detailed numbers that you can come up with, I'll look them over and then talk to my people in Japan and get back to you."

"Great."

As I walked from the car I wondered how expensive this gig would be. Forty million dollars is a lot of money—and that didn't even cover the other expenses.

When I got back to Japan we received a fax from the manager. I looked at the numbers—astronomical numbers—and I tried to pull off the deal, but even during the Bubble forty million dollars was just too much for a single performer at a single concert. Or at least that's what my Japanese partners thought. Our investors felt this was too much risk. We told Stevie we couldn't pull it off. I wish we could have, Stevie is a great man.

Before we left to come back to Japan we thought we had one even bigger opportunity come up. Of course, we were drunk on success and at the time of the Japanese bubble a lot of bubble ideas floated around. Looking back now, we were probably intoxicated on our previous success with Dick Clark—or maybe we were just intoxicated on the cocktails at the Beverly Hills Hilton bar. This deal would have knocked the world off its feet. It would have changed Hollywood, and would have been the climax of my career. Some people thought we were nuts to try it, but we had titanium balls. It all came down to a Hollywood vote...

They say when it rains it pours.

My buddy, Sekiguchi and I were pouring down drinks at the Beverly Hills Hilton Hotel bar one afternoon. We had the best rooms the hotel could offer—huge suites. We were high rollers and we were getting rolled over by the California sun, California girls and of course the California cocktails.

It was just another day on the job.

As we sat at the bar Sekiguchi spoke: "Ya know Rick-san, we got big contacts here in USA and Japan. This is great, it doesn't get any bigger than this."

I sipped my red wine and thought about what Sekiguchi said, "Yeah, it don't get any bigger, my friend."

I then glanced at a television behind the bar, and saw something about an actor getting an Oscar. A bell rang in my head. I wondered if Hollywood ever thought of doing the Oscars in Japan? I'd heard that the Oscars Awards Show's ratings were going down. Doing something like this in Japan would be big. It would be bigger than the American Music Award concert series.

I looked at my friend Sekiguchi. "Seki, can you imagine doing the Oscars in Japan?"

"What?"

I repeated myself. "Seki, we have the contacts, let's bring the whole damn Oscars to Japan."

Sekiguchi must thought I was nuts, but he smiled. "Why not Rick-san, that's a great idea, do you think we can pull it off?"

"Do you think the people in Tokyo would cover the cost?"

"For the Oscars we might even sell Rockefeller Center back to the Rockefellers."

"Great Seki, I'll see if we can get this set up."

I knew the Academy Awards office was only a few miles down on Wilshire Boulevard, but I had no idea of how to meet these guys. I thought about what big names I knew in this town.

Before approaching any of my friends, I called Information. I got the number of the Academy of Motion Picture Arts and Sciences. I called there, and slowly pushed my way up the Academy food chain. I told them what I was doing, and mentioned Dick Clarke and our project in Japan. Then: Boom! I was talking to one of their top people, Bruce Davis.

"You're working with Dick Clark?" Bruce asked.

"Yes, Seki and our Tokyo team are bringing in Whitney Houston, Gloria Estefan and a whole bunch of other singers to do an American Awards Concert series in Japan."

"You're the company that set this up?"

"Yeah, talk to Dick if you want to confirm this."

There was a pause on the line. "And your team wants to do something with the Academy Awards?"

"Yep."

"What do you want to do?"

"It's pretty big, I think we should sit down and give our presentation." I didn't have a presentation, I but figured they would want to see one.

"Can you stop by my office three days from now?"

My heart was racing. Here was the chance. "We sure can."

"Great, I'll have my assistant call you back at the hotel and set it up," said Bruce.

We had three days to come up with a plan.

After the call I looked at Sekiguchi and said, "OK, now we need something to show. We'll need a real presentation."

At the time I was as computer literate as a caveman, but Sekiguchi and I went down to the Hilton Business Center. We explained to the lady there what we wanted to do, that we needed a presentation for the Academy Awards folks and we wanted her to work on it for us.

The lady looked at us like we were nuts. "You're kidding me right?" she said.

I said, "Honey, we're not kidding. We need it done within three days."

The Hilton was my favorite hotel, and the service was always great—if they could do it.

"We're staying in your best rooms here and we need this help. *Do you want to keep your best customers?*"

That last sentence clicked a switch.

"May I have your names and room numbers please? I'd just like to confirm that you are staying here. You don't need the best rooms to get my help. I'd be happy to help you out."

"Rick Roa and this is Mr. Sekiguchi."

She left. When she came back she smiled. "I'd be pleased to help you out with your presentation." We were high rollers. She probably would have helped us even if we had regular rooms, but loyal customers always get something extra. With the help of the Hilton Hotel staff we had our presentation ready in two days.

Sekiguchi and I put on our best suits and arrived at the Academy carrying our presentation. I was always much better at explaining things then flicking slides but I felt we needed something to hand out in case Bruce needed some kind of document to explain it to his colleagues. We arrived on time. Bruce met us at the door. He was very cordial and I could see he was interested in meeting this American Japanese team that was already doing this unbelievable concert series in Japan with Dick Clark.

"Nice to meet you Mr. Roa, Mr. Sekiguchi."

Sekiguchi and I took turns shaking his hand.

"Please call me 'Rick'."

Sekiguchi added, "Please call me 'Seki.'"

"Fine gentlemen, please take a seat. So what is it you would like to do with the Academy Awards?"

I opened the presentation. I stopped at about the second page. It was a good presentation but I wanted to speak my mind rather than recite some cookbook script.

"Listen, Bruce, people worldwide would go nuts if the Academy Awards were done in Japan. Can you imagine all the publicity? We have parts of Tokyo that look like Broadway in New York. Can you imagine all these stars coming to Japan, and having the times of their lives? Doing this in Japan would give you guys the best ratings ever for the show. The press you would get would be mind boggling. It would be big, and it would blow your mind. I've got a presentation here that shows all the numbers. What do you think?"

I assumed that Bruce would think we were nuts, but I was telling the truth.

Maybe Bruce heard that in my voice. He thought about it for a minute or two then leaned across the table. "This may all be true, and it does sound rather interesting, *but do you have any idea of what it's gonna cost to take thousands of people to Japan for these awards? Do you have any idea of the logistics involved and the cost to co-ordinate all this?*"

Bruce gave us this smug look. He had a right to. It was a big job and would cost a lot but I already knew it was gonna be a lot of money. At that time there were Japanese partners who would have given anything to do this deal. I knew I could get the money no matter how much it took.

I leaned over the table and looked at Bruce. I spoke slowly and looked into his eyes. "We're not talking about *money* here, Bruce, we're talking about whether *ya wanna do it or not?*"

Sekiguchi nodded his head in agreement.

Bruce looked at me and his attitude changed a hundred and eighty degrees.

"I believe you, this is unique and interesting," he said. "But the Board of Governors, they are a conservative group. They have already turned down a deal for New York and Toronto."

"This is Japan, Bruce—Tokyo."

"I am gonna put this up to the board and get back to you. No promises but this is *really* interesting."

"When's the next board meeting?" asked Sekiguchi.

"In two weeks, I'll get back to you gentlemen soon after. In the meantime, please pass on my best regards to Dick. What you gentleman are doing in Tokyo is very unique and interesting."

We thanked Bruce and left.

Two weeks later the board voted against the idea. The rumor I heard was that even though it made some business sense, the board did not want to lose the "Hollywood" touch at the Oscars, not even for ratings or money. It was a long shot but hey, we gave it a try. If you're not in the game you can't win.

Hollywood, go figure.

Losing these two deals hurt but we were already working on a big project. People wonder where Japan got all that money back then. For us, our early '90s finances were all tied to the money made in the Bubble Time. One fellow's name was Matsui. Mr. Matsui owned a lot of real estate, including the Alexis Hotel on the Willamette River in Portland, Oregon,. He wanted to be associated with the music awards, so some of the funds came from him. Sekiguchi was helping to sew these seeds. I was helping to harvest the crops. We were a great team.

Along with them there was the Japanese Broadcasting Company known as WOWOW Cable TV network, which was expanding and looking for new promotional ideas. They saw the Awards Show as one of those ideas. For them it was a godsend: a big event to kick off their debut into the larger cable world. This is how you put together a large scale project: identify the ones whose interest it can serve most directly.

The American Music Awards Concert started at the Yokohama Arena. The Kyodo Production Company was signed to do the production work. Whitney Houston knew this production company and it made a big difference in convincing the big stars to join the event. The

Arena was set up for state-of-the-art concert entertainment, so combining that with a world-class production company guaranteed us the best presentation money could buy.

Our line-up was formidable: Whitney Houston, Bobby Brown, Cindy Lauper, Donna Summer and Gloria Estefan, just to name a few. It would be night after night of the biggest American stars of the era.

In the midst of all this celebrity I found a local connection to myself: Cindy Lauper is out of Brooklyn, right where I grew up. When she agreed to participate I was glad that I would have the chance to meet her. Cindy was coming to Japan a few weeks before the Awards show to do some work. Now, at this point she'd agreed to do the Awards show, but we had no signed contract. We had a small conflict here, but I didn't bring it up right away. Instead, while I was in New York on business I approached her manager.

Her manager's name was Wolf.

I said, "Wolf-san, I really want to meet Cindy."

"That shouldn't be a problem," he said.

He arranged things for me, and I met her in the Tokyo Hilton in Akasaka. (It's changed ownership now to the Capitol Hotel). She looked great, and I really enjoyed talking to her. We compared notes about growing up in our borough on the East River. She had stories, as did I. That was what I wanted: a friendly atmosphere.

There was a clause in the contract clearly stating that Cindy couldn't do any work of any kind in Japan until after the concert series. The problem was Wolf wanted her to be on this Japanese TV program which is the height of our New Year's Eve. It's called The Red Against the White. It's an all night competition of Japanese singers, male and female, and at the end they choose the best. Cindy was booked to close the program with a song. But here was this contract she'd just signed saying she couldn't.

Wolf was going nuts. Here, he'd signed her to two events, but ours precluded the other. She had to get a release from us to do The Red and The White. At first I said: "That's impossible." Then the producer of the Red and the White called me for a meeting. I said: "Sure. Come along. Let's have a meeting." He got there upset, but I was ready with a way out. I said to him:

"Look, I can square this with my people, but only if Cindy's appearance on your show is actually made into a really big plus for the American Music Awards."

"I think that's possible," he said, warming to the idea. "What have you got in mind?"

"Well, what we're all worried about is Cindy upstaging her appearance at the Awards by doing your show so close to it. But we can make it work for us. What we need is time for a full plug by Cindy herself promoting our show."

He looked so relieved. "You just want her to advertise the Awards?"

"That's right," I said: "She can appear on The Red and the White. We'll let her do that. But she has to plug our show. She has to do it right at the end of her song."

"We'll give you that," he said, "Right at the end."

That was the moment when all Japan would be watching The Red and the White. And there was Cindy, getting paid to give a free plug to us. That made everybody happy. For us it was at least a million bucks worth of free advertising. An American might think of it like the ad just before kickoff at the Super Bowl.

Most of the contract stuff was boring: nothing but points of law. Let me tell you: never deal with an entertainment lawyer. And I was having to do it in two languages. There's nothing rougher. Take Cindy's situation times-a-hundred and you get some idea. Take something here, give something there. All these demands and conditions have to be translated into that slippery legalese. Then once it's there, bilingual legal minds have to translate it from Japanese to English or vice versa.

It's amazing how much it covers! Donna Summers demanded a bottle of a particular French water sitting next to her when she woke up in the morning. It had to be the exact brand. I had to look all over Japan for that brand; of course you couldn't find it anywhere, so I told her people this.

"Donna's gonna be unhappy…" one of her guys said, threat lacing his voice on every word.

At a point like this I have to give up on reality. I'll look all over the country for a bottle of water, but I draw the line at going global over it. I said as much to Donna's people. "If she's going to cancel over a bottle of water, I can't do much about it," I said. That stopped them.

Whitney Houston was at the height of her superstardom that year. She had just had a string of hits running back nearly ten years, and she was just a year or so away from making that movie with Kevin Costner, "The Bodyguard." There may have been no other artist on that roster that we needed more. Whitney's three main conditions were: One, that she be the first one to appear. Leading off with our biggest star was fine with us, and we'd booked her for the first two nights of the series. Two, she wanted more pay than any other artist there. Certainly we were willing on that point.

Her third condition seemed odd. She didn't want to stay in the Yokohama Resort Hotel where all the other artists were rooming. The Yokohama is a high-end place—you can't do better—but Whitney wanted to stay in Tokyo at the Hilton. At that time it was the only hotel in Japan with connecting suites, and that was what she wanted. The room cost more, and it was over two hours from Tokyo to Yokohama by limousine. That upped the bill even further.

My people and I couldn't figure it out. Why would someone whose shows were in Yokohama want to spend four hours commuting each day? I told Larry Klein and Dick Clark's people: "Do you know how much this will cost?" They said: "She's been in Tokyo before, and that's the place she likes." What I didn't know was that Whitney had a personal manager, a tall strong looking woman, who she wanted to have by her at all times. She wanted this woman's room to be next to hers, and she wanted the rooms to directly connect. This was the only way to make Whitney comfortable. She and her personal manager were that close. You might say Whitney Houston already had a "Bodyguard" well before the movie hit the screens.

But at the time I just kept asking why. I simply didn't have enough information to guess the truth. No one had told me about her personal manager. After some hemming and hawing her people explained the facts of life to me. The reasons behind her demands fell into place. I knew the principle at work here: what superstars want, superstars get.

Though I'd dealt with famous people before, I was pretty amazed by it all. It quickly came to me that I hadn't dealt with this particular breed of fame: international superstars of the music world. But I was learning fast.

Whitney and her special demands brought one more problem. She seemed to believe that she could expect us to keep footing the bill for her suites, her limo, and all the rest for several days past her performance date. She wanted to be there through the performance of her future husband, Bobby Brown late that week, and she thought we should keep paying for her perks. Her manager felt we should too. I said the opposite. We'd contracted for the nights of her performance but that was all. Her manager assumed that the perks of the job included the suite, limo, and other bells and whistles for the length of the concert series, and that was his interpretation of the contract. This produced a conflict in me. I wanted to keep Whitney happy. She was, after all, our biggest star. At the same time I hate to spend money—especially for frivolous things.

This is where one learns to look to at what people want and need the most. Once you know everyone's desires you can strike a compromise. Luckily I had something to work with.

As I've said, Whitney's personal manager was like a guardian to her. One thing Whitney was really touchy about was being alone in her dressing room after the show. She never wanted anyone to come in and see her back there. Her friend, the personal manager, made sure of that. This broad-shouldered Amazon would stand guard outside Whitney's dressing room. Her whole demeanor was designed to intimidate, tall and wide, arms and legs apart, looking like an iron maiden ready for battle. Her eyes told you everything you wanted to know about Whitney's desire for privacy. If she'd been a sign she would've read: "Do Not Disturb—Or Else!"

Then came the man from Coca-Cola. Coke was one of our main sponsors, and this was a guy who'd had some say in that decision. He was responsible for a big piece of the money we were operating on. The Man from Coke had something he wanted too. He wanted to bring several people—people who were important to Coke—to meet Whitney in her dressing room after the show one night. If these people were important to Coke, they were important to me.

But my first reaction was: this won't work. Then I remembered I had cards to play here, and the art of the compromise went into gear. Through her manager I made Whitney an offer: If she would break her no-visitors rule, and let in one of our most important sponsors, I would extend the suite and the limo through the rest of the week. The offer reached the Diva and the Diva softened. After the show that night the Iron Maiden stepped aside. In walked Mr. Coca-Cola and his crew, and Whitney was as nice as could be. The art of the compromise made everybody happy.

The suites, the limo—the whole nine yards—were easy to agree to. We could broker Whitney's concessions on the no-visitors rule. We even agreed to the twenty-foot long wardrobe. What she had was this enormous trunk that she had shipped over here with every outfit she could possibly need. The damn thing was literally twenty feet long, and had as much as you could pack into something that big. Now Whitney played for two nights and she was great. But on the first night she wore a yellow leotard. The second night she wore a black leotard. That was it. But we could give-and-take on all of this. After all, we were at the top of our game, and Whitney at the top of hers. Isn't it amazing what creativity can do when you're at the top?

But there were limits. One night I was called to the hotel parking lot. I got there, and the next thing I knew a guy from the rental service was showing me the open door of one of our performers' limousines. The performer was someone we've all heard of. The car had taken quite a ride. Its insides were stripped. The passenger section had been paneled in rich hardwoods. All the paneling was gone. Somebody had put their foot through the TV. The bar was a wreck, as were the seats.

The man from rental shook his head. "It's a wreck. That whole interior has to be gutted, and replaced."

"How much is it?" I asked.

"Looks like at least ten thousand, maybe more."

The next day I went to the performer's manager and told him: "Hey, our star took quite a ride last night." I described the damage, and told him the cost.

The manager said: "Yeah, well, ten grand—you can take care of that." He thought he had me over a barrel, but that was because he was as careless as his star. He hadn't done his homework, nor had he balanced the books lately.

We held back a large part of each performer's fee. In this case it was fifty thousand dollars, and a stripped limousine was exactly the sort of thing the fee was there for. I said: "Yeah, we can take care of that. It comes out of your money." He didn't like it much, but he had to deal with it. I think most of those stars get mad, but don't remember long enough to try to get even. Of course, they don't have much to get even about.

The entire project was a long, crazy education for me. It was headaches, twenty-hour days, and way too much need for thinking on my feet. But the Brooklyn streets had trained me well, as had years working in Roppongi. In the end, for all the foibles and frustrations, the American Music Awards Concert series was a great time for all. The performers did well, Dick Clark did well, we did well, and most of all the two countries did well.

It was a salute to all concerned.

13

The British are Coming

On Rugby..

I think you enjoy the game more if you don't know the rules. Anyway, you're on the same wavelength as the referees.
—**Jonathan Davies, A Question of Sport BBC TV (1995)**

Rugby is a game for the mentally deficient... That is why it was invented by the British. Who else but an Englishman could invent an oval ball?

—**Peter Pook's Love Nest**

International rugby star Roger Utley was the coach of the Rugby team at the Harrow School. For the uninitiated (as I was) the Harrow School is one of the English Public Boarding Schools. In the States public schools are the free ones where anyone can send their children. The private schools in America are where the rich and powerful send their kids. Some American public schools may be designed for gifted students, but the basic idea is education for the masses. Britain's Public Schools are exactly the opposite. Schools like Eton and the Harrow School are the elite's educational institutions. They are for the children of royalty, or at least of the upper classes. They started many centuries ago, and when Britain was at the height of empire these schools trained its students to run that empire. Statesmen like Churchill and King Hussein of Jordan went to Harrow, as did poets and writers such as Byron. The Harrow School even produced the Nobel prize winning physicist Lord Rayleigh, and the inventor of photography, Fox-Talbot.

The great generals, admirals and statesmen went there, as did the sons of the rich, though, being British, they hated to rely on anything as crude as money. In a society that is still class conscious, these schools are the realm of the upper crust. We Americans would call them "high-end." We'd say they have "class." But these terms don't quite cover it. The American language hasn't come up with a good word or phrase for what these schools are. Let's just say they are: English, and a part of being English is: Rugby.

In 1995 you could've filled a library with all the things I didn't know about rugby. I'd never acquainted myself with its rules, customs, or anything else. I'm sure I knew it was English. I may have known that some other countries played it. I knew there was a ball…was there a bat? I didn't think so…as I say, there was that library full of what I didn't know about it.

That great gap in my knowledge brings me to one Sunday afternoon when I was walking down Omote-Sando, a nice little section here in Tokyo. There I met an old friend, Christopher Haddon, an English guy who was a Harrow graduate. Christopher's father had been a war hero. Christopher had been in Tokyo for some time, and we'd spent evenings drinking together. During those evenings he told me something about his background, and that whole British public school system.

That afternoon Christopher was with two other people. As soon as he saw me he and his friends stopped. He said: "Rick, I'd like you to meet my friends." He introduced me to Michael Liddiard, the bursar of Harrow School ("bursar" in British lingo means Treasurer) and Sir John Akehurst, the Governors-General of Harrow. Sir John had previously been deputy commander of NATO's troops in Europe. Liddiard had been private secretary to Prime Minister Thatcher.

The British always tell you all about their ranks, not because they mean to, but because they can't help it. As I said, they are a class-conscious people, so they tell you their two or three latest titles without even thinking about it. In fact, it might be rude not to. They talk about rank the same way Americans talk about what we had for lunch. But that's not to say you aren't supposed to be impressed. In fact, you're supposed to be very impressed. That's the name of the game. Polite Englishmen walk around all day being impressed by each other's latest ranks and titles, much as Americans impress each other with their cars, or electronic gear.

Having known a few Brits, I knew the drill, and I was properly awed by their ranks, titles, and all the rest. Christopher was gracious and polite, as the English tend to be when they're not in their colonies. Knowing I'm American, he automatically said nothing about my titles or ranks (of which I have none, and if I did I wouldn't advertise it). He just introduced me as his "good friend."

I then invited them to the nearest cafe—they being bloody Englishmen—for Sunday afternoon tea. Well, being Englishmen, how could they turn that down? So we talked, and I got to be friends with Sir John, and Michael the Bursar. After all, I am half English myself, although they weren't too impressed, considering my Brooklyn accent, and the fact that I fracture the English language, as does anyone from my borough. Nonetheless, we got along, and that night we went out to dinner together. Then we retired to a drinking establishment, where we proceeded to drink, and drink, and drink some more. Finally Christopher gave up, and Michael, the bursar gave up, and Sir John—he was "Sir Johnny" by now—and I got blasted, drinking whiskeys and tequilas, and whatever else came to mind.

So at some point he said: "You know, Rick, it would be awfully nice to bring our boys from Harrow over here to play some of the Japanese teams in rugby."

I said: "Really?"

"Oh, yes. You know, rugby is quite a big sport here in Japan as well."

I said: "Oh, yes," and suddenly, through all the alcohol, I vaguely realized that it probably was, even though I'd never paid any attention to it. Somewhere I had a memory of seeing a headline about some local rugby game, and knowing it wasn't the first time. So there was rugby right here in Japan. But what was he talking about? Bringing those boys from Harrow over here for some games? I was drunk, and sometimes alcohol loosens just the right brain cells. This time it loosened the ones between the sports area and my promotional instincts. And there were sparks. So I said: "Gee, if I could put that together would you guys come back this way? We could have tea again, and talk about everybody's latest titles, and have a few whiskeys…"

"Why, Rick," said Sir John. "That sounds like a capital idea. But, of course, if we're to bring the boys over here, there really ought to be a bit more to it than a simple sports event."

I scratched my head. I knew what he meant. With the British, sports are very serious business, but the way they disguise that is with some sort of pretense of "real" serious business. A soccer game is always accompanied by a business lunch; a cricket match is nothing more than an excuse to loosen the limbs in the middle of midterm exams. So Sir John would have to have some important official mission that would be his own if he were to bring forty boys all the way to Japan. Besides, I could tell he wanted something official. After all, he was a Brit, and it was all very much like the title thing.

Well, with Sir John being a general and all, that hardly seemed like a difficult thing to pull off. Finding an official excuse for a general to visit is a no-brainer. But it wouldn't have been good form for me to admit that to Sir Johnny. No. We were engaged in the serious part here.

I probed, he parried. I mentioned embassy functions. He countered with medals and citations. We finally settled on the idea of some kind of presentation: a speech he could give…that would do it. I thought I could arrange for a formal talk before a group from the Japanese Defense Forces. I automatically transformed this into: "I know the JDF needs to hear from someone like you, Sir Johnny." I told him I could probably get him about 100,000 yen for that. That's about a thousand bucks. I was new at this, and I silently wondered if that was enough of an excuse to be truly serious business. I shouldn't have been so concerned. My new friend jumped at it.

I should tell you right here, while I understand the nuances of English rank and title now, my feel for them then was far less assured. In 1995 I was as bowled over by title-with-a-British-accent as any American. I'd never known a "Sir" before. I was pretty damned impressed. After all, this guy's appointments weren't peanuts: a knight to the Queen, and deputy commander of NATO. One showed class, the other competence.

So there we were, sloshed and sloppy, and our deal was pretty much done. But just to make sure I went to the bathroom, got a piece of toilet paper, and wrote the basic agreement on it as best I could. I covered the basics. I guaranteed him 100,000 yen for a speech that I would get him before members of the Japanese Defense Forces "or a group of equal standing." We signed it, and he folded it carefully, and put it in his pocket. Then he looked me in the eye (both his and mine were a little red), and he said: "Rick, if I ever become a general again, I'm going to need you to be my aide."

"I'd love to take that job," I told him. With all that settled I took him outside, and put him in a taxi to his hotel.

About one month later I got a fax from Michael Liddiard, the Bursar. (Just to add a little more rank here: Michael was an ex-RAF pilot from World War II.) He thanked me for a good time, and asked if I would like to bring Harrow's rugby team to Japan to play? Adding just the right amount of class, he mentioned that he was writing from his summer home in Cannes.

Being an American I wondered what the summer home cost. Then I thought: "Rugby...wow...I still don't know a thing about it." So that evening I sat down in front of my TV, remote in hand, and started flipping through the channels for rugby. I found baseball, football, then suddenly I saw a bunch of guys in short pants running around kicking a ball, and I knew: "That's rugby." Then I switched back to baseball.

But, I thought to myself: Harrow is a very famous school. I watched a guy ground out to third. Then I thought: Rugby is big here in Japan. There was a pop fly. Then I thought: So maybe I can make a few bucks here. So I immediately faxed Liddiard back.

"I'm very much interested," I said. "I'll get back to you on this."

Next I went to the Japan Rugby Union. I'd never imagined I'd be going to that place. I said: "I've got this offer here, and I need to know if you guys would be interested."

They jumped at it so fast I had to step back. "Yeah, sure," they said. "We love it."

So I called Liddiard. "I can do it," I told him.

"Why, that's grand," he said.

"Yes, it is," I agreed, "but I need some upfront money for my own expenses."

"How much?" he asked. "Whatever it is, I can pay you a salary for four months to get this thing moving."

"Ok, I'm going to need 400,000 yen, or about $4,000 per month."

Liddiard didn't blink. "That shouldn't be a problem, Rick." He got my bank information, and a week later there it was.

So I put together a team. First I joined forces with an English school which was promoting Harrow with a multi-week course here that summer. There was a guy there who was ideal to help with this. He knew Harrow, and he knew Japan. Then I got my friend, Christopher, since he's an old Harrow boy, and we put together a presentation for the sponsors. What we were selling was space in a top-of-the-line program book that would be available at the games. This program book would be the kind that people would keep on their coffee tables. It was a key part of the financing. I never dreamed how successful we would be. Christopher turned out to be a top-of-the-line salesman, and he helped get sponsors for programs, pants, shirts, and everything else. The program wound up being 96 pages. I made about a quarter of a million bucks out of that alone. This meant everybody was doing well.

When I brought all this back to Japan's Rugby Union, I had to talk to a guy named Shiggy Kono. At this point I hadn't understood how conservative the rugby union was. Though Rugby is played all over the world, it is inherently an English sport. Its customs are those of the old British Empire, stiff upper lip and all that. So even though I was talking to a Japanese guy, the ruling principle was that of the English game. They liked things simple. They didn't believe in flash, glitz, or even elegant professionalism. It was that last thing that got me. Elegant professionalism was what my approach was all about.

The first time I met with Shiggy Kono I didn't know that this went against his style. This was the Godfather of rugby in Japan, and I wanted to impress him with what we were doing. Was I in for it!

I started telling him all about our plan, and our approach. I told him how we would set up the matches, and how he didn't have to put out a dime. I finished by assuring him of our gratitude. Shiggy Kono seemed happy that a school as prestigious as Harrow was interested in coming halfway around the world to play our Japanese boys. He listened carefully to everything, and from his face I thought he seemed receptive. I was thinking: What a nice guy! Then I finished.

He paused, then said: "I want to tell you one thing."

I said: "What's that, Shiggy?"

"You're nothing but a lousy promoter. You're just trying to make money bringing Harrow over here. I know this, and you know it too. But that's okay. If I think for a moment that you're going to make *a lot* of money out of this, I will cancel it the next day."

I looked at him for a moment. There was no kidding going on here. I thought: *I've never had anybody talk to me like that before.* But I had to respect him. He was giving me the warning right at the start: watch your step.

"Alright," I said, but from then on I wanted to be sure that by the end I'd proved Shiggy Kono wrong. Was I in it for money? Sure. A man has to make a living. But was I in it as some kind of gouging shark? No. I knew better. I was in it because it was good for everyone involved: my British friends, the kids playing ball, and both England and Japan. I knew I wasn't going to change this man's mind right then and there. Instead I would create an event that helped everyone involved. That is the job of a truly professional promoter.

Soon I was working with Zen Shirai, the chairman of the Japanese Rugby Union. This man is a great man of Rugby. We moved ahead and started planning. Just as we were putting plans into action Harrow called and invited me to come to England. I would see the actual Harrow on the hill. So I flew there, and stayed at the bursar Michael Liddiard's house on the campus. Michael's wife was charming. We ate elegant dinners, sipping great wines from crystal glasses. We ate like kings, tasting the great food that the English serve. Brooklyn boy that I am, I said to them: "Hey, I think I was born into this. I don't think I'll ever leave."

They took me on a tour of Harrow, giving me every inch of the VIP treatment. All the boys at the school were excited to meet this guy who'd arranged this match on the other side of the world.

All this, and I still didn't know a damn thing about Rugby.

That came home to me about the time I met their coach, Roger Utley. Before I met him Michael gave me some background on Utley. "He's famous," he said.

"Famous for what?" I asked.

"Famous for rugby," the Bursar replied. He may have thought I was kidding. After all, I'd been there for over a day, and the issue of my knowledge of rugby hadn't come up.

While Roger was famous for rugby, he was also famous for over-40 sculling. He was the champion of all England among the elder rowers. We found him sitting in a boat in the boathouse. He was rowing for exercise. Rudolph introduced us, saying "Roger this is the man who will be taking you and the boys to Japan."

Roger stopped sculling. He turned his balding head to me. He had a long, strong shaped face; looked like he'd been hit a lot in games. Every bone looked slightly out of place.

I though: *This man has gone through a lot of rugby.*

Roger was smiling. He got out of the boat and stood up. As he stood he kept going up and up and up. I'm six-one, but this guy had it all over me. Roger is over six-seven. I was looking up at him. He then said: "Hi, Mate." He shook my hand.

They call him "the Gentle Giant", and I could immediately see why. He was the classic case of the nice guy in the huge frame. He said: "Let's go down and meet the boys." We started down a long path. Roger pointed ahead and said: "We're going down to the pitch."

I said to myself: *What's 'the pitch?'*

Roger saw confusion in my expression. He looked down at me, eyeing me, and he said: "You know anything about rugby, mate?"

I looked up at him and said: "Nothing at all."

He smiled, and said: "I figured."

Then I said: "Ok, Roger, let's get this straight: If I'm ever going to learn anything about rugby I'm going to learn it from you, but I do guarantee you this: I've been in the event business for a long time. I'm going to take you and the boys to Japan, and you'll all have the time of your lives. You can take that to the bank."

He looked down at me and said: "I'm with you, mate."

We shook hands again, and I said: "You still have to tell me what a pitch is."

"It's the playing field, mate."

Thus, my short education in rugby started.

I stayed at Harrow for a few days, long enough to meet all the boys. These were boys of the elite, educated strictly, and destined to be Britain's leaders. Just being there was quite an honor for this kid from the streets. They even let me conduct a small seminar in Harrow Hall. This is where Byron stood, and Churchill, and Peel and Parmeston. For four centuries this school had been turning out great men. I stood up there in front of the forty boys whom I was taking to Japan. I can be pretty cynical, but as I stood there looking at these boys who were trusting their fates to me, I realized this was one of the biggest responsibilities I'd ever taken on. This wasn't just some multi-million dollar event. This went beyond money.

It hit me in a way that made me understand that I couldn't fail them. I understood at that moment just how important it was. Even Shiggy Kono might not have realized that I would be put in such a situation. If he had, I'm sure he would've thought that the "cheap promoter" wouldn't measure up. But I did.

Maybe what Shiggy hadn't understood was that I was a father. My son, Justin had made me aware of the stakes involved in boyhood. My own father had left me on my own, relying on my mother, then on my old and failing grandmother to bring me up. In the end I'd raised myself in the streets. But I'd learned not to let that happen with my own boy. He'd gone to good Japanese schools, and he too had played sports—his on a baseball diamond instead of a rugby pitch. But he'd known his father was watching.

All those things came to me as I looked out at these forty elite British boys. I would have to watch out for them a half a world away. So now we had to get to know one another.

It went well. We got along that day, talking and getting comfortable with each other. The boys liked me and I liked them; that lasted throughout the trip.

It wasn't long before they all traveled halfway around the world. Once we were in Japan each boy stayed with his Japanese rugby family. This was an important part of the trip. The English boys and Japanese families learned about each other's cultures. We rented a big bus, and rode all over, seeing Mount Fuji, and visiting cities, and so many of things that make Japan what it is. The boys got to ride the Bullet Train as well. They played well at several schools, winning or tying all but one match. The boys played their last game here in Tokyo's official Rugby stadium.

Of course, Sir John was with them.

Then there was the matter of Sir John, and his necessary mission: the real spark behind the trip. I hadn't forgotten it. I'd begun the arrangements well before his arrival, putting together the necessary pieces. A unit of the Japanese Defense Forces was interested in hearing what Sir John had to say. We negotiated a date and time.

So it was that the day before the main game Sir John gave a full briefing to Japan's men-in-uniform. It was a professional performance, and gratifying to us all. Sir John was an experienced expert, and a fine fellow as well, and I was glad that I could finally help him fulfill his wish—both that of rugby, and that of an official visit in his own capacity.

The last game in Tokyo was quite a production. We even had the British Embassy involved. At that time the British Ambassador's wife was a strong rugby fan, and she attended as our special guest. Among the crowd were some of the boys' families who'd flown all the way from England.

Those Harrow boys won, beating the Japanese decisively. The boys had acquitted themselves on the field as well as off. In six matches they won four, tied one, and lost one. So their trip was both fun and triumphant.

I had arranged a party at the Cordon Bleu Cooking School, where the French chef was crazy about rugby. His name was Martin and he was one of the top ten chefs in the world. He was teaching there. He catered a reception for the boys and their families for free, supplying champagne, lobster, caviar, pate, and god knows what else.

Sir John gave a great speech, as did Roger, then I gave one myself. I started crying halfway through it. I couldn't help it.

The boys gave me a program book signed by each and every one of them. We'd all learned together on that trip, and every moment with those boys had been special for me.

The morning after that, just as they were about to leave, Sir John called me to his room. "Mr. Roa," he said, "What you've done never has, and never will be matched. Our experiences here with you have been among the best of our lives. That goes for the boys, and for me as well." He then opened up his wallet, took out the piece of toilet paper where I'd written my original promise on that drunken night so long before. He wrote: "Paid in Full" on it, and tore it up.

14

A Fish Company in the Philippines:

Ljubljana, Slovenia—A passionate angler at an eastern Slovenian lake caught a fish so big that he drowned trying to reel it in, the state-run news agency reported Tuesday. Determined to land the sheatfish, a type of catfish, the 47-year-old fisherman walked into the lake after hooking it and refused to let go when it pulled him under, the STA news agency, quoted a friend of Franc Filipic as saying. The friend, who was not identified, said Filipic's last words before he drowned were: "Now I've got him!" Police and divers found his body after a two-day search. The fish was not found.

Not long after that, when the World Cup of 1995 was over, the International Rugby Board (IRB) in Dublin passed a rule allowing rugby to go professional. Many in the world rugby community had been advocating this for years, but the IRB had withheld its blessing. Now they finally acquiesced.

This really opened up the sport. Masters International Sports wanted to make a deal with the Japan Rugby Union to send British players to Japan. The Rugby union said they didn't work in the professional area, but they directed the Masters people to me. So Masters hired me to get professional rugby going in Japan.

But between all these things I had one small job. A fish company hired me. This company had a large tuna cannery in the Philippines on the island of Mindanao. They had an office in Manila. It was in a section called McCarthy, a high-end district which is guarded by guys wielding shotguns. The company was introducing a new product: smoked tuna. They wanted me to go to Mindanao, visit their factory, and put together a promotional brochure aimed at the United States. They also needed me to arrange promotion of the tuna at trade shows in LA and San Diego.

It was a normal promotional job except for one thing: I was working in the Philippines for the first time in twenty-seven years. So much time had passed, but in some ways it seemed like no time had gone by at all.

I stayed in McCarthy in a beautiful apartment. There were a bunch of guys there who remembered the old days in Angeles City. We all sang that old song from the Fred Astaire-Ginger Rogers movies: "We're in heaven..." It was back to what we remembered best about the place: the door-to-door high-end clubs. These places might have been expensive to the normal Filipino, but for us they were cheap. So it was also back to wall-to-wall women, with each of us being able to choose any one we wanted. And you can imagine what we did.

Such an experience (deja vu of a kind) could only last so long. Soon it was time to fly south to the source of all this tuna.

Down in Mindanao I stayed in a place called General Santos City. Mindanao is the island that's home to the rebels in the Philippines. It's the kind of place where you never know what's going to happen. We flew down to Davao which is about a three-hour drive north from General Santos City. We arrived in the middle of the night, but there was a driver waiting to take us down to General Santos City. The trip led us down a narrow, rocky road. It was the kind of road most drivers would slow down on, but not our guy. He'd poured lead into his foot. Suddenly we were hurtling through a jet black night at a hundred miles per hour or more. I was scared to death. The road was bad, the night was dark, and we were breaking land speed records. I had to ask why. My driver said: "This is the land of the rebels. If we hit any we have to just keep going. The faster we go, the faster we get there. If we were to get caught on the way, the rebels will either kidnap us or kill us."

On hearing that I instructed him: "Drive faster." What a ride.

In General Santos City they put me up in a hotel. The first thing I heard the next morning was a hand grenade going off. It was a lot more effective than an alarm clock. I ate a nervous breakfast, then went to the factory. There I learned everything I'd always wanted to know about tuna fish.

When we drove back I asked the driver if he'd take a different way to avoid ambush. He said we were doing that as a matter of course, but over the time I was there, we would be limited in the number of ways we could go. I wondered how many routes there were. Those rides were among the most exciting of my life. I could've easily done without them.

Every day we drove down to General Santos City and learned even more about tuna fish. Every evening we drove back a different way. I kept asking my driver: "How many different ways can we go?"

"We've got a new one tonight," he'd say, but I was beginning to wonder. I couldn't see much, but some of these roads seemed depressingly familiar.

Despite all that I had a fabulous time on my return to the Philippines. The people were great. Down in General Santos City we had cookouts, dancing, singing, drinking, and all the usual activities that I'd always associated with that part of the world.

Finally I got back to Japan in one piece. There I got ready to fly to the States for the trade shows where we would feature the tuna. Before I went I called the head of Masters International Sports in England. He said: "As soon as you get back from there, register the company in Japan. You're going to be the President of Masters International in Japan."

I was ready for that. Though I still was no expert on rugby I certainly knew a lot about promoting rugby. Harrow and Sir John had prepared me for that. And Roger Utley and the boys had given me just enough grounding in the sport to seem like I knew what I was doing.

So I took this knowledge and used my Brooklyn charm and closed a deal with the Japanese Rugby Union as the Commercial Agent for the Japan Sevens International Rugby tournament in '96. I then needed a top title sponsor and I got that too: Nike. There I met a guy named Steve Miller who was then their Director of Global Sports Marketing Relations. What an unbelievable guy. This man used to be a track and field star and had been drafted to play pro ball for the NFL Lions. He later coached for the NCAA and won coach of the year five times! I still work with this guy since he now runs the Professional Bowling Association (PBA) as President and CEO. Take it from me; Steve is the *top* sports management and promotion guy in the world.

At Masters I became hooked on the sport of rugby and introduced it to everyone I knew. I converted many friends to this great game. Many of my American friends would come to the game not sure whether they would like the sport but they quickly converted into enthusiastic fans. Who would have thought a Brooklyn boy like me who played stickball in the streets would push a game with funny shaped ball?

It was great.

I stayed with Masters International for three years, mostly organizing rugby events. During that time I became friends with people at International Management Group, the granddaddy of all sports-entertainment management worldwide. They managed both individuals and events.

IMG had developed the modern field of sports agency. The head of IMG Japan became interested in me because I had the famous golfer, Nick Price under my wing. So I called them, and the head of IMG Japan and I had lunch together. We met a few more times in the following year or two.

During this time the nature of the rugby world was changing. Professional rugby was starting to take hold. In the midst of all this IMG made me various offers. Over time we put together an agreement, and

I went to work with them as a senior consultant and advisor. Tuna fish and professional rugby had been a pleasant interlude. With IMG I would get back to the true challenges.

15

The End of the "Bubble"

There are three ways of losing money: Racing is the quickest, women the most pleasant, and farming the most certain.

—Lord Amherst

Anyone who lived in Japan from the early 1980s through the early 1990s knew "The Bubble". It was a bit like the boom of the '90s in the United States, but even bigger. It was a time when money seemed to be everywhere. If you were a promoter like me, going from one project to the next, it made one part of the job much easier: raising capital. I had a good reputation, and as long as that was there, the cash flowed.

Japan changed in essential ways during the Bubble. The social scientists have written reams about the changes. I'm no social scientist, but I can put some of the change on paper in the only way I know how. I'll tell you a couple of brief stories:

The first is just an episode from the present. It's just one of those what-it-costs stories, so I'll keep it short:

The other night we had a birthday party for one of my friends—a men's night out. It's a guy who's been a friend for 25 years. These were mostly Americans, retired military, or businessmen.

We went to one of the beautiful gardens. Then one of our friends took us to the military hotel, then to a hostess club, the One Eyed Jack. They have a couple of hundred foreign hostesses there. We were there for a couple of hours, then we went to a Filipino hostess club, almost as big. This single night, with five of us, cost over $8,000. And that's not at all abnormal. It's become so easy to drop two thousand bucks that you can do it without noticing. It seems like a huge number of people live this way, because all these places are packed. Everybody goes to them.

It's not as if times have suddenly gotten better in Tokyo. It's a carry-over from The Bubble . That was when the Japanese people finally got used to the idea of spending money.

This second story is from those years, and deserves a little introduction.

During the Bubble many of Japan's farmers suddenly found themselves rich. There they were on farms of a few acres, plots where they and their fathers before them had broken their backs for decades growing the country's rice. This began to change in the 1960s and 1970s. Then came The Bubble. Suddenly, with all the spreading of the urban landscape, a farmer would find his land was worth hundreds of thousands of dollars per acre. A farmer selling eight or nine acres became a multi-millionaire overnight. Most of them took the money, packed up their families, and headed straight for the city. They didn't even wait to watch the developer knock their house down.

They were often nice people, usually a mama and papa with the straw hats on, a little bent over from years of planting rice, and one morning they woke up to a whole new world. These poor folks didn't have any idea of what to do with all that money. This wasn't a business they'd built up gradually, or riches they'd grown up with, and inherited. This was the biggest windfall they could imagine. One day they had to toil at backbreaking labor just to pay the bills. The next day they could do everything and anything they always wanted. There the farmer was, his family crowded around him, with all that money staring them in the face. They didn't know what they wanted—at least not right away. The next thing they knew they'd been set loose in Tokyo with a few million bucks to spend. This wasn't just the farm couple. Their kids had money too. After all, how could mama and papa hold on to all of it? A little spare change fell into the hands of their sons and daughters.

It was the kids who made the big splash on the streets. Or maybe the phrase is: big splat. As soon as they had checking accounts they ran out and bought Lamborghinis, Ferraris, or any other low-to-the-ground sports car they could find. A lot of them didn't buckle their seat belts. A lot of them weren't home by midnight. Plenty of them got killed. These farm boys and girls couldn't believe the city. Here they could go right out and buy liquor, cigarettes, and Dunhill lighters, then mix all that with a ton of steel and fuel injection. Take a liquored-up farm boy who's hardly driven anything faster than a mini-tractor and put him behind the wheel of a car that can do one-hundred-and-eighty kph. Press his foot to the gas, then tell him to light his own cigarette...

The cars were their downfall.

The old folks weren't as lethal. The mama and papa went to Tokyo, like they'd always dreamed. They wanted to stay in the fancy hotels, and eat in the five-star restaurants. But these people had never done that before. They'd always lived on that rice farm.

One couple like this came into a restaurant where I often went, Maxime's. It's a high-end French restaurant in Tokyo. The General Manager, Bruno, was a friend of mine, and one night I found him upset and trembling.

He's a very French guy, and with his French accent he started to tell me: "Oh, Monsieur Roa, this never happened in my restaurant before. Oh, it was terrible."

"What's wrong, Bruno?" I asked him.

"Oh, Monsieur Roa-san, I had the most horrible experience with these horrible people who came right into my restaurant, right here, into Maxime's—the best restaurant in Tokyo." He stopped to mop his forehead. "The man...the old man, he had on a straw hat, as if he were still in his fields...and his shirt...only a lumberjack wears such a shirt when he's chopping down trees...and his wife looked like a little hawk...no, like a little pig. Yes, pig. And they came into my restaurant…and they spoke to my staff…and they…they…they had actually already made a reservation, Monsieur Roa-san."

At this point Bruno obviously had to catch his breath, so I interjected: "Hat…shirt…reservation…I understand, Bruno."

"And they sat at a table. They…they wanted to eat! Th-The farmer…lumberjack…whatever he was—he sat with his legs crossed on the chair! Monsieur, I—I'd never seen anything like…I couldn't look at them! I had to go into the waiting room. I almost cried. What will all my best customers think?"

"Bruno," I said, "don't worry. They're just country people. They can't possibly know."

He blew his nose, then blurted: "But it makes no difference. They didn't know what to order. We had to try to explain to them—to tell them what each dish was. But how could they possibly understand what any of it was? They'd never had food of this kind—of this quality—explained to them before…much less eaten it. No matter what you say, in whatever language, it won't help with such people! They can't possibly know what we have here! They sit cross-legged in their chairs, Monsieur!"

As I recalled scenes from American TV's *Beverly Hillbillies*, I said: "What on Earth did you do, Bruno?"

"Monsieur Roa-san, we had to bring each dish out to them, to show them, so they could see what it was! As if we were in some kind of cheap cafeteria where the food is sitting out in plain view."

I wanted to laugh. But instead I said: "Bruno, this is just terrible. What are you going to do?"

"I'm going to take action," he said. "This wasn't the first time, and if I don't do something it may not be the last."

"What's your plan?" I asked.

"I've told my staff to screen our reservations. There are certain names…names that are much more common out there on the farms. We won't take those names unless…unless we know the people personally. I've told them to only take reservations from the better hotels.

I may require a reference for someone's first reservation. I must do it, Monsieur Roa. You do understand, don't you?"

"You bet I do," I said.

I felt deeply for my friend. It was sad to see a poor, harried Frenchman having to turn away perfectly good money, and I know it hurt him. But, Bubble Time or not, Bruno was stubbornly determined to hold on to his standards. Being French, he could take a certain pride in such arrogance. It was one of those many tests people underwent in those years.

Maybe there was some good in the Bubble bursting. Maybe we needed to come back to Earth.

This next, and almost last story is an introduction on how I started to work with some very beautiful women. I'm not talking about the many beautiful women that you can see every day at the shopping malls or beauty salons. I agree that these women are beautiful. I personally think my wife is the best of them all. I am sure many men would agree that they have the prettiest girl in the world at home. What I am talking about are the women sexy magazines and TV shows show as pretty. Some of these women spend years trying out for these roles. Some do what we call *soft porno*. These women are trained to turn on the erotic engines of men. This story is about that engine moving full steam ahead.

One Sunday morning in 1999 I got a call from my boss Dick Alfred at IMG in Tokyo. I picked up the phone from bed. I was half asleep. I gave the Japanese hello, "Moshi-moshi...*hello?*"

"Good morning, Rick. This is Dick. You have time for brunch today?"

I looked at the clock wondering: Why the hell is my boss calling on a Sunday?

"Brunch? Sure, what's going on?"

"I'll tell ya later. Meet me at the American Club for brunch at twelve."

"Sure—see you at twelve."

I hung up the phone, got out of bed, showered and went to the American Club. This is a great club. At one time it cost almost $50,000 to become a member. Now with The Bubble blown it's about two million yen, or about $20,000. It's still the top club. All the top international execs and US Ambassadors to Japan use it.

I entered the Tokyo American Club and went to one of the most luxurious Sunday brunches found in Tokyo. I found Dick all dressed up in his snazzy preppy attire drinking wine. Dick is in his 60's and always looks like he's just finished sailing.

"Good afternoon Dick," I said, sitting down at the table.

"Good to see ya Rick."

I ordered tea from the waiter standing nearby. "Dick, what's up? I assume it must be *important* to interrupt my Sunday."

Dick smiled. "Rick, how would you like to run Playboy Japan?"

"Run Playboy? What do you mean?"

"Take over all their licensing in Japan. Meet the movie folks, magazine folks and grow the business in Japan. Become the Playboy Japan Director of Licensing."

I thought I had died and gone to heaven. I would have paid Dick to run that project. The guy running the licensing for Playboy Japan got to meet hundreds of gorgeous girls. That person would be invited to all the big parties. I thought about my answer for about a millisecond.

"I'll take it."

Dick put down his wine. "Wait a second Rick, I haven't explained the contract yet."

"I'll take it Dick."

"Cut it out Rick. You need to review the deal and think about it."

The waiter came with my tea. I looked over at Dick and knew some deals did not need a lot of thinking. I knew Playboy's reputation. This deal would open doors to other work for the firm and me.

"Ok, Dick. I'll think about it." I sipped my tea and put it down. I smiled, and said: "Dick."

"Yes Rick."

"I thought about it, I'll take it."

We both laughed. He knew I would do the job for free. I did look at the details later, but they were just that: details. The job was mine.

As the Japan Director for Playboy's licensing I wanted to kick off something big. I put on my promoting hat and kicked some events into motion to get Playboy more business. One of those events was a Hugh Heffner art exhibition. Hugh had collected a lot of great art over the years: Andy Warhol, LeRoy Neiman and art from the early Playboy magazines. This early art is worth tons of money now. I set this up in the same part of town where I'd met Sir John and the Harrow School folks. I used a real classy coffee shop known as the Anniveraire in Omote-Sando Tokyo.

I pulled over a million-and-a-half-dollars worth of Hugh's art out of its Japanese storage bins. It was a kick ass bash that became a total success.

Later while working with the Tokoho Shinsha, the Japanese company doing the soft porn in Japan, I was asked to escort Playboy's Japanese Millennium Twins from Peru, back to Japan. I'll tell you, they were knockouts, and they were great to work with.

Experience like this didn't hurt at all when I started working with the most famous sisters in Japan. They are the famous Japanese Kano Sisters. I became their international manager at IMG and worked to promote their careers. I'd love to talk about the Sisters but I don't want to destroy their important ingredient for success in Japan: Mystery.

In the next chapter I'll talk about a near death experience and a person who saved my life.

16

A Brush with Death and a New Life

They do not love that do not show their love.

—William Shakespeare

About five years ago I wanted to get married again, so I asked my wife for a divorce. There was some question as to whether she would go along, but I decided to try to work things out on generous terms. Nonetheless the question still hung in the air.

I wanted a quick divorce. Divorce can be tremendously complicated in Japan if either party wants it to be. In Japan one in three marriages ends in divorce. In the States it's a coin flip. In Japan if one party contests the divorce the couple has to go together to a family center, to see if they can work it out. You have to talk about it with your spouse and a counselor, perhaps several times. I saw no need. We hadn't lived as married people in over twenty years.

I had communicated to her that, with Justin grown, I had no reason to send her money anymore. He was still living with her, but he was also making good money on his own. I knew this concerned both of them. To calm those concerns I offered her a generous monthly settlement. At first she resisted. But because we hadn't really lived as man-and-wife for years, I knew she had no real claim. So I gave my son the papers. I told him that she must accept the settlement, or take me to court, where proceedings would take years, and she'd probably lose. "Tell her that," I said. "It's a generous thing I'm offering, and I'm happy to do it, but if she takes me in to court I won't give her anything." She understood the sense of that, and I was glad she did. She had been a good mother, and I didn't want the situation to become difficult. In the end our agreement was good, and fair, and was in keeping with the Japanese system.

The divorce went simply. Once I had her consent I was able to get our divorce in America, where the legal process was easier. When I had her signature on the papers I took them to San Diego, California. There a judge looked at them, and granted the divorce. I could take this route because all those years before I'd had the good sense to marry her in the American Embassy. An embassy is considered to be a part of the nation it represents. A marriage performed there was technically performed in America so now I could divorce her in America as well.

The divorce enabled me to marry my present wife, Machiko. Machiko worked here in the area at one of the most important hospitals in Japan. A nurse herself, she managed the entire hospital nursing staff. I don't think I'm being at all prejudiced when I say she is quite beautiful.

There is no comparison between my first marriage and my second one. To put it simply: the first failed, while this one succeeds every day. Machiko keeps me healthier than I'll ever deserve to be. She watches what I eat, what I drink, and she helps me by arranging so many of the details of my life.

But how did I find such a woman? And how could this guy, this Brooklyn boy, this King of Roppongi you've been reading about, deserve such a woman? The answer to the second question is a mystery to me. The answer to the first is not. That's what this chapter is all about. It is the story of my brush with death, then my coming to life with Machiko.

About five years ago I went from Masters International to the International Management Group (IMG). Going with IMG was a part of my transition to a more normal life. This wasn't so much because the work was different. It had more to do with the incredible things that happened in my private life at about the same time that I was making the move into business.

In my last year at the Masters I was out every night. I smoked a lot, drank a lot, and I was out until two or three in the morning. I had plenty of girlfriends too. I was hanging around with a bunch of guys who were all doing the same thing. I'd been doing this for a long time, but it had accelerated in the past few years. I'd go out, and hit the entertainment areas every night. I never took a break.

In my last year with Masters we had a conference in London about future projects. The conference lasted several days, and on my last night there my colleagues took me to a club on St. James Square. It was like a hostess club, but there were only two drinks: champagne and soft drinks. A lot of Indian women worked there.

We drank, drank, and drank some more, all the drinks being bubbly. We must've gone through forty bottles of champagne. The next morning I woke up in my hotel room. I was due to leave that afternoon, but there was a complication: I woke up next to an Indian woman. I had no idea how she'd gotten there. I looked at her and thought: "What is she doing here? And why do I feel like I do?" God, I was hungover.

I finally got her up and out. I took some aspirin, and got my head together as best I could. I packed my bags, and took a cab to the airport. My flight back was bad. I slept a little, but there was no escape from the hangover. I arrived back here. After all those hours I still felt as if a truck had run over me. With all the jet lag following me, I knew I wouldn't sleep. I decided I should go to a club and have a few drinks. I went to a place called Magumbo's. I sat in there and drank tequila shooters. I left the place feeling good. I went home, went to sleep, woke up about seven, and I said: "Why do I have all this pain?" It was bad enough that I felt like I'd better go to the hospital.

Now, a long time ago, when I was growing up, I remembered my grandmother saying: "If you're going to go to the hospital make sure you've got clean underwear and clean socks." So I went in to take a shower. While I was showering the pain got so bad that I almost started hallucinating. At that point I left the shower, and headed for Sanno Hospital. It was close by.

I got there about eight in the morning. The hospital wasn't even open yet. A woman doctor came over to me and asked: "Is anything wrong?"

I must've looked like hell. "I have this terrible pain," I told her.

"Come on with me," she said, looking in my eyes. "We'll do some tests." They took my blood, then left me in a chair alone while they checked it. The pain got worse. I started hallucinating again. I fell down on one knee. All I knew was pain. It was all I perceived. It was the kind of pain that overrode everything. I was aware of someone whispering through the hurt. I heard a voice tell me: "Mr. Roa, you're a very sick man. You can't leave the hospital."

The next thing I knew I was on a gurney being wheeled through the corridors. Then there was a white light shining into my face, and something poking my stomach, then my chest.

The pain stopped when the lights went out.

Finally I woke up with two needles coming in one arm, and two needles in the other. The pain had gone away but I still didn't know what was wrong with me. I was groggy, and I felt terrible. Then I passed out again.

Magically I awoke with Justin standing by. He said: "You're alright."

"No," I said, "I'm not alright. I hurt. And I don't know what all these needles are." Then the magic show ended.

I passed out again.

The next time I awoke the doctor was there. This was a doctor who'd given me physicals. He said: "Mr. Roa, you're a very sick man, but fortunately you will live."

"You mean I might've died?" I demanded.

He nodded. "Yes."

"Doc, what happened to me?"

It turned out I had acute pancreatis. My pancreas had swollen, and had nearly burst.

The doctor told me this then said: "Mr. Roa, you drink a lot."

"Well," I said, "not a lot. I like to have a drink or two in…"

"You drink a lot," he confirmed. "And you smoke a lot."

"Well, only in the evenings."

"You do," he said.

We analyzed my situation and came up with this: I was ten kilos overweight, and had been for quite awhile. I was a social alcoholic. But though I'd almost died, I was lucky. My luck was in the fact that I'd gotten a curable disease. It might've been a heart attack or cancer or a liver problem. This was something I'd recover from pretty quickly.

I was being fed antibiotics and fluids. I wasn't allowed to eat.

The doctor told me: "You have to quit drinking and smoking right now. If you don't you'll die. You have to lose weight and get more sleep. You have to accept the fact that you're in bad, bad physical condition."

From that moment on I didn't smoke or drink. It was cold turkey. It's not so hard to do when the alternative is death. When you realize that, it's amazing what you can do.

The worst thing was not eating. It drove me crazy. Nurses were always coming in changing my needles. They started in my arms, but I had to do this for awhile, so soon they were doing my legs, my feet—all kinds of places. I got so tired of needles. I wasn't used to any of this, and I hated every minute of it. I felt like all those young girls—the nurses—were using me as a guinea pig. So I bitched and I moaned, and bitched and moaned some more, and though I was losing the weight I needed to get off, I was driving everybody crazy.

The nurses were more patient with me than I was with their needles, but after awhile enough was enough. So they followed hospital procedure and went to the Chief Nurse about me. They told her all about this pain-in-the-ass up on the fourth floor. The Chief Nurse came up to visit me, to see if she could calm me down. When she got there I was reading the paper. I looked up at her, and it was love at first sight. She sat down. I said: "You're the best looking nurse I've ever seen." And I said to myself: "How can this beautiful woman be a chief nurse? I always thought chief nurses were broad-shouldered, big-muscled female wrestler types."

I think she kind of liked me from the first, but mostly she just wanted to calm me down, and stop me from being a son-of-a-bitch to all her nurses. She talked to me for awhile, and got me to promise to be a little better.

I made it into a deal with her. "If I'm going to be in a better mood, you've got to come back and visit me sometimes."

She nodded, saying she would.

To myself I said: "I like this one very much. She's a doll. How can I get to her?"

She did come back and visit, maybe more than she would've with other patients. There was time for it because I was stuck there for over a month. As much as I'd hated it at first, now I didn't mind it too much. Still, I couldn't eat. After a couple of weeks they started giving me little bowls of cereal, and tiny pots of rice. Now and then they gave me a banana. This was breakfast, lunch, and dinner combined. So when she came around I said: "Isn't there any way I can get some real food? I'm beginning to feel like a monkey." Finally they gave me a potato.

After several weeks they let me go home, but still I had to come back once a week for testing and antibiotics. When I first walked out of there I was actually gaunt. But I felt like a new person: I'd quit smoking and drinking, and I'd dropped about ten kilos. There was also this woman. I didn't know what role she'd played, and I wasn't analyzing it.

When I'd go back each week I'd get the antibiotics in a drip that lasted an hour. I would always demand: "Where is the Chief Nurse? I want to see the Chief Nurse!" I would repeat the lines a few times to make sure my point got across. Now the hospital rules forbade the nurses—especially the chief nurse—from fraternizing with the patients—especially patients like me, who had such a reputation with the ladies. But I managed to get her phone number. I started calling her and asking her to break those rules. At first she wouldn't, but finally she said: "Yes."

She had Sundays off. She said she'd meet me in Omote-Sando where everybody meets everybody. This is a chic part of Tokyo where I had met the Harrow folks years before. I took her to a museum. They were having an exhibition of pictures from Yugoslavia. This was my attempt to show her I wasn't a drunken nut anymore, and I did have a little culture about me. Afterward we went to a restaurant. She made sure I was eating the right food.

One thing led to another, as they often will, and we started getting serious, but then we had a big fight. It was my fault, of course. I wanted to make up, but couldn't get a hold of her, so I went to her house at four in the morning when I knew she'd be getting ready for work. I banged on her door, and yelled I was going to break it down. So she let me in, and somehow that did it: she knew I was serious. And I captured her.

She moved in with me. I was still married, but only in the most technical sense. I hadn't lived with my wife in twenty years. So after awhile I took care of that and Machiko and I were married. It was a wonderful wedding. We had many friends attend including writers and TV personalities. Japanese personalities Kyoko and Mika Kano attended the wedding. It was extremely kind of the Sisters. Little did I know that one good friend who attended our wedding, Tony Teora, would soon be talking me into writing this book. Machiko and I were the happiest people in the world to see so many friends attend our most important day.

Machiko and I moved into a nice place. We got along, and with her there I didn't want to drink or smoke. It all added up. Working at IMG was a more stable position, with a much more sedate lifestyle.

I hadn't worked exclusively for one company since the '70s. I'd always been a freelancer, but I adjusted well to my new job.

Machiko kept her nurse's job until just recently. She helped the Sanno hospital build a larger, better building up the street from where they'd been. She was truly instrumental in that, and it put a crowning touch on her professional experience.

Machiko is originally from the country, but like so many Japanese women, she came to the city and learned a profession.

Nursing is one of the lowest paid jobs in Japan, but it is also one of the most respected. She had incredible respect, and still has it. She also worked very long hours, and never looked at the clock. She never walked, she always ran. I knew that if she kept this up for too many years she would know nothing but her work.

Finally I asked her to stop. At first she didn't. For two years I got after her to quit. I had some selfish motives, but mostly I was concerned for her. I couldn't help but feel as if I needed her in my life more. I said: "You should realize your value. You need to take a break, and see who and what you are." Well, she thought about it, and thought about it, and finally after two years she decided to try it.

Last October she said: "Ok, I'm going to quit." I was shocked. She said: "I'm not necessarily retiring for good, but I am going to stop working for quite a while...six months or a year."

She went to her boss, and of course he tried to get her to stay. He said: "It's that husband of yours, isn't it? He's talked you into this."

She said: "Well, of course he wants me to stay home."

In the end it wasn't easy for me to get her to slow down because the people around her really understood her value—as do I.

They had so many going away parties for her...she got beautiful cards and presents. We looked at them, and I said: "You see, they wouldn't do this for just anybody." She was truly touched.

Finally in December she took a real vacation. We first went to LA for our vacation and then we went to Acapulco for Christmas and New Years.

When we got back here after New Years it was really like the first moment of a new life. Imagine you have a bird cage, a beautiful little bird, and that bird had been in the cage for as long as anyone could remember. Then all of a sudden you open up the cage, and say: "You're free." And the bird looks, and sees, and looks at you with eyes that ask: "I am? I can fly?" And the bird steps up gingerly, maybe rustling her little wings a bit. Then she peers out, getting her first peek at freedom. Then she jumps out, spreads her wings, flaps, and wobbles a little bit. Then she takes flight. At that moment, when she feels the wind beneath her wings, there is nothing more beautiful. There's my wife.

Now she's trying to do all the things she couldn't do when she was working sixteen, eighteen, twenty hours a day. She got a driver's license, then she grew her nails long—things she'd never been able to do. She went to the hairdresser, and got her hair done a different way every time. She painted her toenails, wore perfume, wore makeup—She'd always been beautiful. Now she's even more so.

She's also made a much more domestic home life for me. I love that. What man wouldn't? She's a good woman, and I love her madly. Can I say more?

Epilogue:
If I Were a Young Man:

You cannot discover new oceans, unless you have the courage to lose sight of the shore.

—Andre Gide

If I were a young man coming into the working world today, I would go to Shanghai. It's like Japan was thirty years ago. It's a driving place, buildings going up right and left, money pouring in, and everything's getting capitalistic. Shanghai has a long history as a commercial center. After fifty years of communism people tend to forget that, but it was. For decades the Bank of Shanghai was the commercial center of Asia. I think that's something that lurked just below the surface all these decades, and not all that far below the surface. Now they can be all that and more again, and I think they're going to do it.

Not that I think there's anything wrong with Japan's future. This country has had some rough sledding since the end of the Bubble, but it's coming back up again. There's nothing at all wrong with Japan for a young man. But here he'll be building on a huge structure that's already in place.

In Shanghai they've been waiting to get back to capitalism and all it can do since before World War II. In fact, in many parts of the country they've never experienced any kind of modern capitalism. Now they're doing it, but they're just starting. That's where a young man can make his own niche.

I'm a maverick and always have been. At my age I fit in fine with the Japanese system. I've carved my own niche within it. My whole life has been here for thirty-five years. It is here that I've had my triumphs, and here that I've made my mistakes. I have no deep regrets, only a few mild ones.

I still work. I don't go at it like I once did, but I am older now, and I can enjoy all parts of life at a deeper level. I can enjoy my beautiful wife, who has made my life so worthwhile, and my son, who is making his own way in life. A man can ask for little more.

I have my own place in this world, and I'm comfortable in it.

But if I were a young man today I might have a harder time here than I did. I was lucky to have arrived at the right time. It was a time when the abilities of an American maverick could be accepted here. I'm the nail that sticks out. That was a good thing to be when I first got here. I looked around, and saw all those holes in the ground. They needed something to fill them. The Japanese had their system, they had their way of doing things, and I admired it. But they were also building a whole new nation. That takes people from different places with different attitudes. I like to think I provided a little of that for my Japanese friends, while they gave me—and keep giving me—an exciting life in a land that is always both old and new. I've been a part of Japan's great growth. I'm the American who came, looked and found the right place to make my name.

It's been pretty good for a boy from the streets of Brooklyn.

About the Author

Tony Teora lived in Japan from 1994–2004. He currently lives in La Jolla, San Diego. He has known Rick Roa for many years. "Rick's life is so mind-boggling and heart-warming that putting it together in the *American Maverick in Japan* was like riding a jet roller coaster through downtown Tokyo with your best friend." Tony Teora is a science fiction writer and an entrepreneur in the computer industry. To see other books from Tony Teora please see his website at <u>www.tonyteora.com</u>. You can also email Tony Teora at: Tony@ TonyTeora.com.

0-595-31428-7

Lightning Source UK Ltd.
Milton Keynes UK
13 October 2009

144894UK00001B/349/A